What Lead

I'm captivated by Shannon's story, challenged by his witness, and moved by his resolve. As I read, I found myself turning the pages quickly and anticipating what was coming next. Shannon sounds a clear call for leaders of the church in rural America—but the principles translate to any leader trying to move a congregation toward life change in communities of all sizes. This is a rare book ... one that I'll be buying several copies of to hand out to encourage pastors every chance I get.

Tim Stevens, Executive Pastor
Granger Community Church

Author, *Pop Goes the Church*
Co-Author, *The Simply Strategic series*

twitter.com/timastevens
www.leadingsmart.com

I believe in Shannon O'Dell and his book because he leads with vision and heart. His vision is not a dream about something he has never experienced, but his vision is coming into reality as he is transforming church in rural America. His heart is sensitive to God's Spirit because he is a man committed to the Bible being his model to reach his world with Christ. If you want to believe again, if you want to know again that God can use you and your church, read this inspiring work and let God take you to a new level of faith. Share this book with spiritual leaders across the country and there is no telling how many leaders that will once believe God can use them, right where they are.

Dr. Ronnie W. Floyd, Senior Pastor
First Baptist Church of Springdale
and The Church at Pinnacle Hills, Arkansas

twitter.com/ronniefloyd
www. ronniefloyd.com

The lies about churches "in the boonies" echo loudly throughout the landscape of our culture. And too often, leaders believe them thinking "success" is reserved for places with big populations and bigger budgets.

But in *Transforming Church in Rural America,* Shannon O'Dell confronts some of the most powerful and prominent of these lies head on. And as he shares his passion for what church is meant to be, he reminds us of the truth that God can move anywhere—even in rural America.

No matter what size church you are a part of, this book will challenge your traditional thinking, force you to look beyond the status quo and enable you to grasp a bigger vision of what God has in store for your ministry and your leadership.

Ed Young, Pastor
Fellowship Church

Author, *The Creative Leader*

twitter.com/edyoung
www.edyoung.com
www.fellowshipchurch.com
www.edyoungblog.com

Shannon O'Dell's passion for the rural church in America is contagious. The vision to see the small church reach multitudes through partnerships with other churches is a move of God, and *Transforming Church in Rural America,* is right on the wave of God's plan.

Craig Groeschel, Senior Pastor
LifeChurch.tv

Author of *The Christian Atheist: Believing in God but Living As If He Doesn't Exist*

www.lifechurch.tv
swerve.lifechurch.tv

I've been friends with Shannon for years; he's an awesome man of God! I would encourage pastors, staff in the church, and leaders to read Shannon's book. I've watched him take a *dead* Church in the middle of nowhere *and grow* a great Church. It's awesome!

Ken Freeman, Ken Freeman Ministries
www.kenfreemanministries.com

No one in America knows more about reaching people for Christ in a rural setting than Shannon O'Dell. He and his team at Brand New Church are literally changing the world one small town at a time. *Transforming Church in Rural America* should be on the must read list of anyone who is serious about going into the highways and byways and compelling them to come in.

Geoff Surratt, Pastor of Ministries
Seacoast Church, Charleston, SC

twitter.com/Geoffsurratt
www.geoffsurratt.com
www.seacoast.org

If you want to know how to bring life to places that desperately need it, then you have to read *Transforming Church in Rural America,* as Shannon O'Dell shares about the great risk he took in building a church in the middle of rural Arkansas; an endeavor that, I have to say, has been nothing shy of successful!

Rick Bezet, Lead Pastor
New Life Church in Central Arkansas

twitter.com/rick_bezet
www. newlifechurch.tv

Shannon O'Dell shatters the "rural reality" with the power of vision, excellence, and technology to prove no matter how small or low on finances, your church can become a relevant force for transforming lives today.

Tony Morgan, Pastor of Ministries
West Ridge Church

Author of *Killing Cockroaches And Other Scattered Musings on Leadership*

www.tonymorganlive.com

Shannon O'Dell isn't just "Breaking the Rurals" – he is shattering the rules for ministry and blazing a trail for pastors in any size church and any size city in America. A visionary leader with a passion for people and a zeal for the local church, Shannon's amazing story will challenge your thinking about the way church has always been done.

David Anderson, Lead Pastor
Crosspoint Community Church

www.blog.moviepastor.com
www.crosspointlive.tv
twitter.com/moviepastor

Being a church planter in rural America, (Rolla, Missouri) I have seen and experienced many things that Shannon details in this book. The application of the principles in this book will take strong leadership driven by a God-given vision. The results will bring about transformation to churches in rural America that have neglected the Great Commission and allowed church to be more about them than about those needing a Savior in our communities.

Eddie Jones, Lead Pastor
Christian Life Center

www.clcrolla.com
twitter.com/eddieljones

transforming church in RURAL AMERICA

breaking all the RURALS

Shannon O'Dell

New Leaf Press

First printing: March 2010
Third printing: January 2014

Copyright © 2010 by Shannon O'Dell. All rights reserved. No part of this book may be used or reproduced in any manner whatsoever without written permission of the publisher, except in the case of brief quotations in articles and reviews. For information write:

New Leaf Press, Inc., P.O. Box 726, Green Forest, AR 72638

ISBN: 978-0-89221-694-9
Library of Congress Catalog Card Number: 2010923398

All Scripture quotations in this book, unless otherwise noted, are taken from the New International Version of the Bible.

Cover Design by Diana Bogardus

Printed in the United States of America

Please visit our website for other great titles:
www.newleafpress.net

For information regarding author interviews, please contact the publicity department at (870) 438-5288.

New Leaf Press
A Division of New Leaf Publishing Group
www.newleafpress.net

Contents

Acknowledgments

Let me say a word of thanks:

To my gorgeous wife Cindy—This project is a tribute to your faithfulness to Jesus Christ. Your obedience and Christ-walk is my prod and push to be more like Jesus.

To Bruce Medley—For believing your church can be an influence for rural communities all over the world. Thank you for resisting the urge to settle.

To Dad—Thanks for listening to me when, as an 18 year old punk, I told you about God's call on my life. I will never forget sitting in that McDonalds booth and you telling me, "Son, if you are called, then go be the next Billy Graham."

To Brand New Church Staff—For being my arm lifters and vision casters.

To the true report card of my ministry: Anna, Evan, Sara, and KJ—You are my disciples and I love what I see. I love you.

To Tim Dudley, Laura Welch, Todd Hillard, and the amazing New Leaf Team—Thank you for believing in the mission of reaching rural America in a relevant way.

Foreword

Are you aware that sixty-percent of all the Protestant churches in the United States of America average sixty people or less on a weekend? Great numbers of men and woman are strategically positioned in the little towns and villages and hamlets at crossroads all across the country—deployed as if by divine and sovereign decree. They occupy these places of great potential.

I wonder what might happen if every local church, every congregation and every pastor in all of these rural communities, would light up, ignite and catch fire? What would happen if they would catch, not a man-made substitute, but the fire of God from the hand of God and the altar of God and the spirit of God? What might happen?

I believe many do not try because they have been convinced it can't be done. They have never seen it done. They have never heard of it happening. But then, from time to time, God lights someone up on fire and He invites someone of great faith to dance the line which is the sharp and cutting-edge between insanity and faith… to dance that line and walk by faith to do a new thing…to create and innovate.

And I have seen that in Shannon O'Dell. It is the witness of a faithful servant of God, like Shannon, that transforms so many of the rest of us. There is nothing new under the sun—but occasionally we need to see a man or woman of God who tries a new thing that is so far from what we have imagined that we look—and we gasp—and in that gasping moment we realize this is something only God can do.

That was my experience when I sat in a crowd listening to Shannon talk about the way he was distributing the message of the Gospel through rural America by using a Hummer and satellite dish. A collective gasp went through the room.

First, because we thought, "What in the world?" And then we thought, "Oh my, what would my people say?"

What a moment—to experience someone who manifests the reality of consequential living! We look and we see that this person stretched, and stepped, and tried a new thing, and lo and behold the old old story was wrapped up in a new new package.

The story didn't change, but the method did—and it was creative and innovative, and inspired each of us to try something new. Your new thing isn't necessarily putting a satellite dish on a Hummer. (Don't suggest that to your board. You will be calling U-Haul!)

But friend, I'm telling you the idea that somebody might try something that's innovative and creative—that inspires me! And I want to think outside the box, and I want to imagine what might happen. What if I took the lid off? What If I didn't say, "I am trapped by what is and what has been?" What if I dreamed a God-sized dream? What if God gave me today the dream that I have been praying? What if God satisfied my prayers and answered my prayers? Are my prayers too small?

"Show us a way, O God, to reach our community," doesn't get prayed often enough. "Give me courage, give me faith, grant me wisdom for the facing of this hour in my community," is often left out. We don't pray those prayers because we've got other concerns—smaller, more pressing things. It's time for a God-sized dream. And a God-sized vision.

And so, this foreword ends and the book begins with a prayer. I pray for Shannon, and in so doing pray for rural America. And I ask you to agree with me in this prayer for Shannon and for the pastors of rural churches across this country—many who think what they're doing doesn't matter; many whose loftiest goal has been diminished to hoping that the gate keepers at the church don't yell at them anymore.

Oh Father God, we pray for Shannon O'Dell, for his family, for his marriage, for his ministry, and for his congregation. We pray for his witness and we pray for his mind, that he will think new thoughts and dream new dreams. We pray for his body that it will be healthy and strong, that he can run long the race that you have set before him.

We pray for his friends, that they will be true to him and true to You; that they will always lift him up, always encourage him, always help him on the journey. We pray for resources to flow into his ministry because it is Your work and what You have purposed to be done. We believe that You will resource what You have commanded to be done. And so we pray that people with money will give money, that people with time will give time, that people with faith will exercise their faith, that people with big ideas and big dreams and big visions will give those ideas and dreams and visions to the cause.

I pray, Father, that Shannon will encourage and challenge pastors and leaders in rural churches all across this country. I pray that the God-sized work you are doing in Arkansas through Shannon's ministry will be repeated in towns and villages in every corner of our nation. In Jesus name we pray for this. Amen.

Mark Beeson
Senior Pastor, Granger Community Church
www.markbeeson.com

transforming church
in RURAL
AMERICA

breaking all the RURALS

Part 1

BEGINNINGS

Then he said to them all: "If anyone would come after me, he must deny himself and take up his cross daily and follow me" (Luke 9:23).

1
POSSIBILITIES

Rural Realities and God Possibilities

Where is the wise man? Where is the scholar? Where is the philosopher of this age? Has not God made foolish the wisdom of the world? (1 Cor. 1:20).

The "Unwritten" Rural Rules:

- ⤳ Successful churches grow in thriving urban or sprawling suburban America.

- ⤳ Sparsely populated rural communities are behind the times and not worth our time.

    Cities are strategic; the country is inconsequential.

    The best, most visionary pastors are hired by growing visionary congregations.

    Rural churches can only afford the leftovers from the leadership pool.

    If you want to be a "successful" pastor, go to the cities.

    If you want to drive a minivan with 200,000 miles on it, go to the sticks.

Those are "the rules" about the rurals — the unspoken but clearly understood values that permeate American Christianity's beliefs about churches in the boonies. Oh sure, no one would say them out loud — at least not in public — but don't tell me that the vast majority of us don't believe those rules, because, well, I did, and so did everyone around me. I accepted "the rules" hook, line, and sinker. But that was six years ago. Today I have only one thing to say about that: Forget the rules!

Where would thoughts like that come from, anyway? From the God who desires that none should perish? From the One who leaves the 99 to find the one? From the Son who had a carpenter for a dad in a town with a population of less than 500? No way. So if the rules didn't come from the Way, the Truth, and the Life, they could only ultimately come from the one who steals, kills, and destroys. No doubt the rules are messages sent from the pit by the liar, and today I say it's time to send them back unopened, stamped "No Such Address," labeled "permanent delivery failure"!

Listen, God loves rural — no question about it. Most Old Testament prophets were called from a small town. Jesus was born rural and grew up rural. When the invitation to join Him at His banquet table fell on indifferent ears in the cities, Jesus invited small-town people to His party. "Go out to the roads and country lanes and make them come in, so that my house will be full" (Luke 14:21 NIV 1984).

Don't get me wrong. I love what God is doing in the metropolitan areas of the world. Most of our mega-churches, TV ministries, and "known" churches are found in larger cities. But let's be honest: churches in the cities that have populations of hundreds of thousands or millions of people should run attendance of thousands. But when God does it in the sticks? When He defies our entrenched church-growth models and gathers seekers and worshipers together en masse in the middle of nowhere? Well, that's when you know God loves rural and that He loves breaking the rules, and that we have nothing to do but worship Him and thank Him for doing the impossible.

I didn't believe that before. I now believe in a God who can do a work in towns of hundreds and still reach thousands. I also believe that the lessons we are learning out here in the rurals could be oxygen and nitro in the burbs and urbs — fuel that could explode in more heavily populated areas — if only someone would provide the spark. Yeah, God loves rural, and so do I . . . at least I do now. My hope is in God and my belief is in the Holy Spirit's movement in rural America and small communities of the world.

Passing by the small farms and little communities each day on my way to the church, I am reminded how this was a vision God held for me. I could have never imagined what He was up to, and so I really resisted at first — almost missing the ride of my life because of the "rules" I believed about "the rurals." The fields I pass, the scattered houses and barns and tractors . . . each one reminds me that this is a field, a mission field, and arguably the greatest mission field. I personally believe that rural America is one of the most over-churched, unreached people groups in the world. The number of church buildings says nothing about the state of Christianity in rural America. We find church buildings on most street corners in small towns. The prairies are dotted with churches everywhere. *But that is part of the problem.* These struggling churches won't survive the next decade if they cannot grow, and rural churches have challenges unique to the ministry, especially if they are passionate about their family's church heritage (but are not passionate about the mission of Christ) or have great desire but little faith, their vision limited by what they can see, not by Who is unseen.

And here is why: because rural America is perhaps *more churched and more unchurched* than any place on earth. When someone becomes a Christian in China, Uganda, Nigeria, UAE, or in Saudi Arabia, they take the Bible, see it, trust it, and believe every word that is written. You take the Bible to some churches in rural America and there is a tendency to assume ownership of it as if they wrote a portion of it — yet so few read it, so few believe it, and so few follow it. Yes, rural people come from rich church heritages — but so few have experienced the living Cornerstone of the Church, and so the buildings and the congregations are dwindling, falling into disrepair, collapsing.

But that's not the way it has to be. A great harvest for Christ is waiting in the heartland and rural communities of America, and in that harvest are the seeds to reach the world. The people out here in the rurals are strong people, smart people, dedicated people. They are people who know what it means to work — who "get the job done" because they know they must. They know that "if it's broken, it must be fixed" (whether it's 5:00 or not). I'm telling you, in the rurals we know how to make it happen with bare hands, baling wire, and determination. So not only is it a mission field, but it is a field of the best missionaries, too . . . and I tell you this from experience.

In 2003 Southside Baptist, after 50 years of ministry in a town of less than 100 people, was barely surviving with 31 attendees and an annual budget of less than $45,000. Today we are doing business as "Brand New Church" — and for good reason. At the moment, about 2,000 people gather with us in person. Another 1,500 are registered attendees of our iCampus (joining us from 177 different countries like India, Nigeria, Kenya, Ghana, Spain, South Africa, Norway, Saudi Arabia, and the Philippines). In the last nine months, we had 63,933 online visitors, and we ministered to another 40,000 through

BNC Global Outreach, and we are rapidly launching satellite churches using, of course, real satellites.

There are days that I sit stunned and wonder: *How did I go through all that? How am I still doing it? I know there is no way on God's green earth that I should still be doing this.* And to be honest, I'm as blown away as anyone. I know where we came from, but in any given moment I'm rarely sure of where we are, and I'm just going with the flow when it comes to the details of where we might be headed.

It's been an amazing journey. By God's grace and plenty of blood, sweat, and tears, we have climbed to some of the most amazing mountaintops and navigated through some of the most unimaginable valleys. In the pages ahead, it will be my humble privilege to share some of the details of our journey with you, a journey that has solidified five key goals of rural ministry into our branding: Vision, Attitude, Leadership, Understanding, and Enduring Excellence. When this level of "V.A.L.U.E." became our reality, our story as a church jumped into light speed.

But please know that this story really isn't about us and our church; it's about you and your church. We all share a common journey in this world. As believers we have always been and always will be connected and dependent as members of the greater Body of Christ, as congregants in the

Pastor Shannon O'Dell (top, right) with the BNC leadership team.

Church. More than ever, this is true in the digital age where followers of Christ across the globe or across the pasture can connect with the click of a mouse.

So ultimately, it's not BNC's story and it's not your story; it's our story, and as such it is an invitation; an invitation to join together and share our tears, our fears, and our resources of vision and hope as we take to the roads and country lanes of America and the world, as we live out the invitation to join Christ at the banquet table. By God's grace, we've been on an amazing journey — one that, by His mercy, may be only beginning, and may be beginning together.

In the following chapter, I provide not only details of our struggles and growth as a church, but videos and links to information that I pray will bless you, your family, your ministry, and your church. These will be scattered among the story of our journey and continuing mission to give God our very best. A helpful listing of the links will be provided in the appendix at the back for easy reference.

I remember the day I lay in bed and bawled my eyes out because I was praying, "Jesus, please don't send me to rural America." But that was a long time ago, back when I used to believe that there were rules about the rural church.

No more.

Now I believe this:

It's time to break all the rurals.

2
COUCH

One White Couch:
Answering the Call ... Finally

Whether you turn to the right or to the left, your ears will hear a voice behind you, saying, "This is the way; walk in it." Then you will defile your idols overlaid with silver and your images covered with gold; you will throw them away like a menstrual cloth and say to them, "Away with you!" (Isa. 30:21–22).

"Leave your country and your people," God said. "And go to the land I will show you" (Acts 7:3).

All was well in the buckle of the Bible Belt. I was serving as a youth pastor in Oklahoma City under an awesome pastor in a great church. Kids and parents thought I was the best. My wife and I and our four kids were comfortably settled in the suburbs, and I was making, with benefits, almost $60,000 a year. I was traveling to about 11 countries, and the whole world felt within my grasp.

I had served as a student pastor for 11 years, casting vision and discipling students to become engaged Christ followers. Surrounded by like-minded comrades in a well-entrenched suburban Christian sub-culture, I was on track, toeing the line, and life was good. The bottom line is that it was Cush City — and I don't mean in any way to dog the call God gave me up to that point, but the truth is that I had a cream puff job. We had 70 staff members around and I could "hide" at a foosball table and a ping-pong table better than anyone. Not physically hide, but get lost or go essentially unnoticed in the crowds of people and non-stop activity of a large and thriving church.

Sure, everyone was happy and content and it all looked like "success," but whatever it was, it had nothing to do with my vision, my personal walk with God, or passion for Christ. Yet because the building was big, the budget was big, and we were drawing in big numbers of kids and families, people automatically thought I was a worthy authority. I wasn't faking it, but I'm not sure I was very real either. Little did I know that it was all about to change . . . in a big, little way.

Getting Real

In the spring of 2001, I sensed God's call to lead a church. The voice of God's Spirit was clear, and, to be honest, it really made sense. I was starting to age out of youth ministry and (like multitudes of youth pastors before me) the next professional step was to seek an associate or senior pastor position. I clearly felt that God was leading toward a senior pastor position. Without advertising that I was even looking, people started telling me about opportunities in metro communities, and I started receiving offers on almost a weekly basis — and they were *good* offers. I had paid my dues, earned my reputation, and now it was time to move up to the big leagues — like a first round draft pick in the NFL. Sweet.

Then in October the phone rang.

"Shyannon Odeyell? Bruce Medley in South Lead Hill Arkansawwwwwwwww callin'." I knew Bruce from the old days, and he knew my family well. My hometown wasn't far from where Bruce was calling; it was just south of what people would describe as Sticksville and north of Nowhere. I listened politely as Bruce told me about a small church in the tiny Arkansas community that was looking for a new pastor. I understood what he was talking about all too well. Small town? *Been there; done that; got the T-shirt; moving on.* Man, after high school I put that place in the rearview mirror and never looked back. To return would mean moving 500 miles and what felt like 500 years in the wrong direction. It might as well have been halfway around the world . . . no, scratch that, it was *farther* than that. World missions would have been far less of a stretch than a rural church because that was the very last place I felt God wanted me to be working as a pastor. Out of respect for Bruce and to spiritualize my response, I reluctantly said I would pray about it.

Honestly, I didn't — didn't pray about it, that is.

I laughed to myself instead. *My vision, my calling, my future is not in the boonies,* I happily thought to myself. *Maybe near Dallas, or Nashville, or Atlanta,* but I was positive it was not in South Lead Hill, Arkansas. *No one* had a future in South Lead Hill.

Because I was on staff with a Southern Baptist president for several years, offers kept coming in and I was holding out for the best one. Looking back, I can see that my desirableness had nothing to do with integrity or spirituality. It had nothing to do with anything other than because I was in a large church and people wanted their church to be large, too. Everybody wanted that; so did I. In America, to go from a thriving metro fellowship to a struggling rural church is considered probably the most stupid professional move you can make. Cindy and I had received calls from some of the most unbelievable churches in America. They weren't senior pastor positions, which we believed God was calling me to, so we were not able to say yes to those, but we had opportunities. To be a senior pastor, to cast the vision for a local group, to be the local shepherd for a church organization — it was my call. I felt called to a senior pastor position in a large metro suburban area — to minister in established or thriving middle-to-upper class America. Period.

So I kept praying for God to just show which direction and urban area He wanted me to be living on the fringes of. Since South Lead Hill was farther than half a state away from a large metro area, I dismissed the opportunity almost as soon as Bruce called me, and I went about my way. The idea was so far "out there" (literally and figuratively) I didn't even fight it. It was not an option I even considered. I had a wife, four small children; it just didn't seem to make sense for my ministry, my family, or me. I shrugged the whole thing off and moved on.

But Bruce kept calling. I continued to say I didn't think I was the one God had in mind for them. I even sent some of the most radical videos from my time as a student pastor to prove I was just "too out of the box," too radical, too over-the-top to be considered. But when Bruce found out I would be in my hometown for the holidays, he asked if I would just come by the church for a few minutes and meet with the search committee. *No harm in that,* I thought. *Let's get this over with so ol' Bruce will give it a rest.* I already had my exit strategy before I drove into the little parking lot. I would go in, say hi, be polite, and I would then gracefully spiritualize my decline, saying I "felt led" to another area.

When I pulled up to the church, all my worst fears and assumptions about rural churches were confirmed. The parsonage was decades out of date, in disrepair, and filled with mouse droppings. The little church had problems of its own. The parking lot was dirt, with the exception of six parking spots that were memorialized in the concrete. There was only one bathroom, unisex that is, on the upper floor. The pews and carpet were green. The lobby was small with the Sunday school attendance board reading dismally, as well as the giving. Inadequate sound, old upright piano, stains in the ceiling, and the darkest paneling you have ever seen. The church smelled musty . . . you know, like old churches smell — a symbolic scent somewhere between formaldehyde and moth balls. *Shannon, you have real vision,* I reminded myself, *and this ain't it!* I sat through the meeting, answered some questions, and cordially told them, "Thanks, but no thanks." They responded by asking me to come and give a candidate's sermon on January 12. *Sheesh. These people just don't get it. Don't they know that my no means no?!* I thought to myself, never once considering that it might be God unveiling His vision for me.

I went and gave a sermon on January 12. But I'm telling you, I pulled out all the corks. I was sure that I could convince them that an off-the-wall, alternative-tending, emerging-leaning, over-the-edge youth pastor was not what this sleepy, traditional fellowship and town needed. So I let them have it . . . all 25 of them who showed up that morning.

My message was entitled "Becoming a Person of Passion." I shared why I thought the church is passionless today, because so many are involved with Christ but not committed to Him. Quoting Matthew 9:36, I shared how their passion must start with a heart that breaks for those who need to be rescued. I told them about Evan Roberts, a 25-year-old coal miner who shared a message after a Wednesday night service in 1904 to 17 people, exhorting them to:

- confess every sin known to God
- remove every doubtful habit from their lives
- obey the Holy Spirit's prompting, and
- go public with their witness for Christ.

In the next 30 days after Roberts' service, 37,000 came to know Christ; 100,000 became believers in the next five months. The revival surged through the colleges, cities, and coal mines. I told them what Roberts said about it all afterwards: "God has so made man, that whenever anything fires his soul, impossibilities vanish."

I talked about embracing the same attitude as Jesus Christ, who left His heavenly stature and came to earth as a bondservant of men. I even went a little bit charismatic on them, exhorting them from 1 Thessalonians 5:19 to not "put out the Spirit's fire!" I told them how spiritual fervor, not human wisdom, must direct our intentions. I told them, "Don't settle for good intentions, but God-led intervention. Don't settle for good activity, but accomplishment." And above all, I told them they must be obedient to the call of God. I finished it all off by quoting Jim Elliot: "God consume these idle sticks in my life that I might burn up for Thee."

As I walked away from that musty little building that day, I knew that I had blown them out for sure. I had played their game; I had toed the line for a hopeful family friend, and I was sure that they would agree I was not the man for this job. As I drove home, I was sure I was leaving the hicks and the sticks in my rearview mirror for good. (What I didn't know was that the sermon I had preached to them was the same message I needed to hear the most myself.)

None of my plans to avoid living in South Lead Hill were working out, and it was looking more and more like I was being invited to this small church in a small town in the middle of nowhere. It was time for desperate measures. I decided to throw out some fleeces — a lot of fleeces — nine to be exact. I made Gideon look like a joke with the length of my list. I insisted that an addition be built on the parsonage. I wanted health insurance. I wanted to eradicate all committees and build ministry teams instead. On and on I went. I was confident that there was no way this little church could or would accept my terms and conditions. And that's what I wanted, of course. I was

31. For a 30-something pastor, rural America is just not cool. It's just not vogue to go to a place with a monster steeple, stale carpet, and ten families of 60-plus-year-olds that are looking to bless the pastor with a blackberry cobbler.

Metro America was calling me; it was better for my family, my ministry, my vision (as well as my pride and reputation, I kept telling myself). I wanted what Bill Hybels and Ed Young had. Nothing wrong with that, but the idealized ministry and church had become an idol in my heart and mind — a gold- and silver-plated image that was taking the place of God in my soul. My fleeces were a desperate attempt to protect my "idol" as I hoped I could have both God and the church I dreamed of.

It didn't work. That little church agreed to every one of my requirements. Yep, each and every one, approved with no problem.

In a revealing conversation with my wife, I realized God had been laying the groundwork for this move to South Lead Hill in her heart even while I was resisting it. Still, I lined up all the reasons one more time why this was a ridiculous idea: not enough people; it is rural, *really* rural. No money in it. No security in it. No leadership. No vision. . . Add it all up and there was no way that church could grow. So I just went back to where I was and waited for the ideal — until one day, months later, when I took a nap and God revealed His plan for me.

The White Couch

It was November 26, 2002. I was in Mississippi at my in-laws' for Thanksgiving. Good food, good family, and the traditional "wow, that was a huge meal" syndrome. I snuck away from the small talk toward a side room to loosen my belt and sleep off that last piece of pie. No one ever goes in that room, but somehow I ended up there lying on my mother-in-law's white couch. (Who has a white couch anyway?) I kicked up my feet, stretched out, and dozed off. . . .

I am going to tell you right now that I have written more sermon series in my dreams than when I'm awake. I woke up from a dream one night and said to my wife, "Babe, write this down: CheeriO's—Obedience, Obscurity, and Obligation." We wrote down all these O's that we have to be cheerful about and I turned it into a series of messages. I know that's not the norm, and some of you are probably back-peddling a bit, wondering if I haven't gone over the edge, but all I can say is that I seem to be more receptive to God's leading when I'm asleep rather than awake — and sometimes He speaks very, very clearly. That day, on the white couch, was one of those times. I heard God whisper, "Shannon, what if I want to use you to blaze a trail to pioneer a work in rural America? What if I want to use you to do that?"

Up to this point, I had considered South Lead Hill an invitation — and not a very attractive one at that. I had pawned it off by thinking that this was just an overly determined little church that was unwilling to take no for an answer. They were inviting me, but that invitation was an option, just like an invitation that someone might get inviting them to a party. But after the white couch, I knew that everything was different. This was not an invitation. This was a call. And a call from God is not an option. So many of us are guilty of confusing God's call with an invitation. It's not an invitation; it's a command from heaven. Over the years I had seen many people negate their call to marriage, to ministry, to their family, etc., by convincing themselves that it was a "take it or leave it" proposition. And I've seen them do it with very grave consequences.

I woke up on the white couch and sat down with Cindy, telling her that I believed God wanted us to pastor at Southside. She gasped and said, "No way. I couldn't live in that parsonage. I couldn't put our kids in a small town school system. Are you serious?" I told her how and what God had spoken, and we both began to weep. We knew it was going to be a lot of work. We knew it was going to be difficult. We knew we were going to be frustrated, and we knew that we would have to pay for it in many different ways.

That call from the couch should have been enough, but Cindy and I had thrown out one last fleece — one I was sure could never be done in a million years. We told the church we must receive a unanimous vote to accept this pastorate. The church's history indicated clearly that this would not take place. It was our fleece out of God's will for our lives. The church had an attendance of 31, but even so, how often will everyone in a church agree to the same thing? Especially when it comes to choosing a pastor? The odds on this one had to be in my favor.

The vote came back 31 yes and 0 no.

God's call had come — and we answered it.

Visit **www.nlpg.com/bnc** *and watch the first video, "The Call."*

Join me as I re-visit our original church building and share important insights on God's call for your life and ministry.

No Refrigerator Magnets

Cool things happen in churches for most people when they announce that they have been called.

One of my friends felt God's leading to a rural village in Senegal, West Africa. When he told his friends and family about this call, they wept, cried, and celebrated. The local churches began to pray for him. The denominational convention supported him financially, funding not only a comfortable salary and retirement account, but making sure that they were covered for their education and processing expenses as well. They spent about $10,000 to send them off with an inspiring commissioning service. They sent him care packages, prayer letters, and made it a priority to include him and his family on the Wednesday night prayer list. I thought the support they gave him was just awesome; it was much-needed financially, spiritually, and emotionally. As a final display of enduring commitment, hundreds of families put prayer magnets with my friend's picture on their fridge to remind them to pray for this missionary family.

When we announced our call to South Lead Hill, people laughed. They laughed as if we had told some sort of joke. Some just shook their heads, trying to make it compute. Family and friends looked at us with furrowed brows. "Why are you taking a huge pay cut?" "Why move your family to the middle of nowhere?" They sat there and said, "Oh, dude, that isn't a good move financially; that is not really wise for your family. Where are your kids going to go to school? How can you do this?"

In the end, no one gave us a red cent to go. We never made the Wednesday night prayer list. No one stepped up to send us care packages. No one sent us off with a commissioning. And, significantly and symbolically, we never did end up on a refrigerator magnet.

Because of the rules about the rurals, I'm afraid that this response is all too common for the rural pastor and his family.

Southside Baptist Church in South Lead Hill, AR (population 93)

Yeah, we say that we support rural pastors, and we verbally affirm the importance of what they're doing . . . but do we really? When rural pastors come and go, we usually smile politely, pat them on the back, and walk away just really thankful that we don't have to do what they do where they are doing it. If a man is going to North Atlanta or the Grapevine, Texas, area, everyone understands that and everybody gets behind it because it makes sense. But if you get called to the sticks of Arkansas, people think you are a freak or destined for obscurity and status quo.

It's hard to describe the rainbow of emotions that we felt during those days. I felt like I was wearing overalls at the country club . . . we had broken the rules and we just didn't fit anymore. It wasn't all bad to be sure, but in many ways we felt patronized, marginalized, misunderstood — and alone. I guess no one should be surprised when the call of God leads him or her first into the deserts of loneliness. Moses went there, Jesus went there, Paul went there . . . other men who have followed God's call have walked there. Why should I have expected anything different?

When we finally accepted the call — when it finally soaked in that it was going to happen — my wife and I cried. We bawled. God called us to rural America. We knew it was our calling but we wept. We would leave Oklahoma City and our church of 4,000. We were going to South Lead Hill, Arkansas, population 88 — and we were going alone.[1]

---

1. Just so you know, it doesn't have to be this way anymore. Sure, we might be isolated geographically, but there's absolutely no reason that we can't be networking together as pastors of churches in small communities and sharing resources, encouragement, wisdom, and vision. We don't have to do it alone anymore. You'll hear more about this in later chapters, but if you want to, go ahead and log on to brandnewchurch.com and let's get connected, now.

3
DESERT

Desert Days:
Finding a Place in Nowhere

For I am about to do a brand-new thing. See, I have already begun! Do you not see it? I will make a pathway through the wilderness for my people to come home. I will create rivers for them in the desert! (Isa. 43:19 *NLT*).

I slowly walked down the small, dark, and narrow hallway, past the unisex-only upstairs bathroom, and slowly pushed the door open. A mixture of anticipation and reality made my stomach feel funny. The carpet and paneled walls were decades old and worn; the computer, the desk, and the chair were dinosaurs in their own right. The bookshelves were full of old hymnals, old church training material, dusty cassette tapes of messages from previous pastors, and VBS material. This was the perfect picture of what I knew would be the passions of the congregation I was to lead. This was my "new" office. This is where it would all start.

We all know that rural churches face dwindling attendance and aging attendees. With young people making plans to be anywhere but church come Sunday morning or Wednesday night, these churches are on a steady decline. Struggling to keep the doors open, small churches do not have funds for large and aesthetically correct buildings or even the remodeling of an old building. That's their reality. Now it was my reality. I plopped down in the squeaky chair, took a deep breath, and surveyed the surroundings. *"What now, Lord?"* It was Day 1 at Southside Baptist, and I had found the way to my own "backside of the desert." I knew that we had much, much work ahead, but where to start? *Sunday, I guess. Let's start with the Sunday service.*

Go to **www.nlpg.com/bnc** *and watch "Day One" as I describe the challenges of our first days in ministry at South Lead Hill.*

The first day, or even the moment when you know something needs to change, is an opportunity to be expectant about God moving in your ministry.

It's Sunday, But Monday is Coming

I had gotten a sense of Southside Sundays when I had done my candidate's sermon weeks before. On most Sundays, there were 11 people in the choir and about 26 or so people in the congregation. About one-half of the congregation in the choir would be the dream of most music directors. Our minister of music did everything she could to make it the best, but it was a struggle . . . kind of like herding cats. For starters, the organ player was completely deaf. Seriously. He could not hear at all. He was the nicest guy (God rest his soul, he earned it), but he and the music director would have to give head nods and hand signals to stay on the same beat, because this poor guy had no idea where she was at. When his song was over, she would look at him, give him the signal, and they would try to cut off the song together.

Logistically, there were other immediate concerns regarding the music. After I got up to pray after the hymns, I would say, "Amen," and the whole choir would get up and shift to their seats in the pews. It took forever, and they would make so much noise I don't think anybody ever heard the first 20 minutes of my message. The transition probably would've gone faster if they had sat down just anywhere, but each of them had their own seats, unofficially reserved, and they all had to sit in the same place they had for who knows how many years and decades. Force of habit inadvertently got in the way of the quality of the service.

And then we had technology issues (our "technology" consisting of two microphones and a tape recorder). We needed to make recordings for the church members who were shut-ins at a nursing home, but initially I was the only one who knew how to push the right button. So I would ask the music director to pray at the close of every song set. That way I could get up and run to the sound booth at the back of the church and hit the record button. We had a "sound man," but I'd always find him lying down asleep — every Sunday. They had built this really nice sound booth so he wouldn't be disturbed by the service, I guess. So anyway, I'd run to the back, hit the button, try not to wake the sound guy, and then run back up the aisle hoping our music director hadn't finished the prayer yet so I didn't get caught in the rush of choir members heading for their pews. I always hoped I wouldn't accidentally take out the organ player, because he couldn't hear me coming and it was a real tight little aisle about as wide as my hips.

That's where we started; that's what happened every Sunday.
I would jump up on the stage and think, *God, is there any way
on earth this place is going to grow?* (We did grow that first week,
though, from 31 to 33 — a remarkable 8 percent growth!)
No doubt it was a very sobering start. If the past 50 years had
taught them anything, and if those first weeks had taught me
anything, it was that change would not come easy, naturally,
or randomly. If things were to change, we would have to be
intentional, and God would have to be faithful. I learned right
away that if you want to go somewhere else, you have to start
where you are, and God is ready to meet you on the backside of
your own desert. But at the same time, we, as leaders, must be
willing to make the four most difficult decisions required for a
rural pastor who desires to see the church go to the next level:

Four Most Difficult Decisions for a Rural Pastor

1   To pastor in Rural America . . . with low incomes,
    low resources, and low expectation

2   To reach the lost and unchurched. (Most people say
    they want to reach the lost . . . until they do and then
    the church starts changing!)

3   To equip the church with accurate and healthy
    structure . . . changing bylaws, constitutions, and
    church policy as necessary

4   To remove "Holy Cows" to be more effective . . .
    such as pews, property, and people

We had faced the first decision after the "white couch
incident." We had packed up, charged ahead, and were jumping
in with both feet. But the other three decisions were still ahead

of us. How do we do it? How do we proceed? As I pondered these questions, God spoke very clearly to me again: "When you desire to grow a congregation, you will never get it. But if you grow congregants, then you are going to see transformation in their lives and within the church." It was one of the most important distinctions of my journey. In all my thinking before South Lead Hill, I had wanted to grow a big congregation. But that was putting the cart before the horse. I realized I needed to be focusing on growing individual congregants, not a big congregation.

When we were about six weeks in, I was getting frustrated with the lack of participation. I finally realized that the congregants were not capable of doing the job because they did not have a passion for Christ — and I finally realized I really have to love people. Throwing down some creative relevant talk wasn't going to change their lives. I had to lead with my life. So I started by sharing the gospel. I had the opportunity to lead a guy to Christ, then I led another guy to Christ, then another guy to Christ, and all of a sudden life transformations were happening. I can't tell you how huge that was. When a person has been churched and *then* they're changed? Genuine transformation communicates big time in a small community, and it started to get everyone's attention. The church started growing.

Then I started casting a vision for what I desired to see. I started introducing iworship once in a while, or I would flash a PowerPoint slide up on the screen. Everyone thought I was Houdini. Wow, how did he do that? In about a year we were running 90. It was awesome! I mean, it looked like the place was packed. According to the deacons, we could seat 275 people in the building. But I did a test one time and tried to put seven people on a row that supposedly would seat nine. Not a chance that was going to work. I determined that the building could only seat about 180. So when God grew that congregation to about 200 people, I had this great vision to build a building — a real building. It was a 1.1-million-dollar plan and would seat about 400 people. *Pretty impressive in a town of 88,* I thought. That was a powerful vision.

Just one problem: it wasn't God's vision.

The process of bringing this building to reality was slow and painful. We paid an architect and went through some of the most unbelievably boring planning meetings — I'm talking verbal chloroform. The big discussion was where to place the breaker box. Week after week we debated. I just about went nuts, but that's the way we had to make decisions because that's the way the church was structured: *everyone* had to vote on *everything.*

During one business meeting there was a guy who had investigated what type of coffeepot we should get now that 90+ were coming. So several prayed and fasted about it (sorry, a cynical exaggeration to illustrate the energy and focus on one insignificant decision) and then discussed it for at least two months (no exaggeration at all). In the end they picked a handsome three-pot Bunn coffeemaker. Motion made, seconded, and all in favor ready to say "Aye" when a lady raised her hand and said, "I just don't feel comfortable having the word 'bun' on our coffee maker." I was stunned. I said, "It doesn't say 'buns.' It just says 'Bunn.' " I knew that she had read *Left Behind* and didn't have a problem with it. (Wouldn't it have been awesome if they had made the sequel to that *Right Behind?* I would have loved that, no buts about it.) Anyway, God be praised, she dropped her concern so we could move on without making a motion to amend the decision. I'm telling you, though, I was getting impatient. I know that most churches have their own versions of the breaker-box-Bunn-battles, but I, for one, was getting very annoyed with it all. But again, I knew I wasn't just invited here — I was *called* here, and that call superseded my annoyance.

When that was all going down, we also instituted a student ministry project. We wanted to do something big and rowdy for all the kids, but we didn't have the space. So we made a proposal to the deacons: if we get more than 60 kids coming on Wednesdays, can we remove the pews and replace them with stackable chairs so the youth could use that area? Only seven students were in the church, so I'm guessing nobody took the proposal too seriously. They said, "Sure! If you get over 60, then we'll pull the pews out." We voted on it as a church and in a unanimous decision, all agreed. Little did they know, a huge, huge sacred cow was on its way to the slaughter.

Southside had rabidly protected its sacred cows before, I would learn. They had once voted down a sand volleyball court that the pastor wanted to build to draw in more kids from the neighborhood. They voted it down because someone had memorialized the dirt that had been brought in to level off a potential parking lot. No joke. Memorialized dirt. But that was nothing. Our pews were like most rural churches' pews. They had little plaques on them, memorials to deceased and beloved ancestors whose memory and honor lay etched in the little strips of brass. Why did they agree that we could take them out? I'll never know for sure. Maybe they never thought it would happen; maybe they were reluctant to make a stink about it in the moment. Everyone seemed to be on board, but in reality, I had just lit the fuse on a time bomb.

Take a moment and view "Change = Conflict" at **www.nlpg.com/bnc.**

It's not always easy to implement change in your ministry at a church with deeply ingrained traditions. Change often means some conflict, but change is vital in fulfilling God's call in your life.

Brick and Mortar Blessings

Meanwhile, I was still trying to plow ahead with my vision for building a new church. Step by tortured step we were making some progress. We even had a ground-breaking ceremony. But we were still arguing so much on where the breaker box was going to be that the whole process had backed up. *Every* meeting they would come to debate it. I know you think I'm joking but I'm not. Then God, in His infinite mercy, in His own perfect timing, revealed *His* vision for our church.

Down the road apiece, Elixir Baptist Church was struggling to keep its doors open. They were down to about six attendees, about $17,000 in debt, and had been unsuccessful in recruiting a new pastor (a situation that many rural churches face). "Would you take over our building that seats about 125 people?" they asked. They were doing what so many rural churches need to do: give in without giving up. Elixir was willing to "give in" to another area organization that would allow them to "go on" and flourish and succeed. We took that opportunity before the deacons: what if, rather than building, we expanded to two campuses? Amazingly, the idea sailed through. When it came to a vote, it was clear to all that God's hand was in the matter. He had provided a building for nothing and saved us not only from our sins, but also from further breaker-box debate. Furthermore, it was a huge step up in the population base we were serving. The church was about nine miles away in the metropolis of Bergman. They had a real restaurant and even a gas station, population: 472.

A Little Mud on the Bylaws

Vote by vote we were making some progress. Even before we added the second campus, the church was really, really growing. God was truly blessing us. But more than ever, I was realizing the need for a biblically accurate church leadership structure that would allow us to move more decisively and more quickly. We had survived the breaker box, but when the parking lot almost killed us, I realized that we were seriously stuck in the mud, literally. The ground outside the original church was a soggy, muddy mess when it rained. In our meetings we discussed and debated and proposed solutions, but before anything could get done, we were not only knee-deep in mud but up to our ears in subcommittees. *Somebody could have just ordered a truckload of gravel five months ago!* I thought. But we couldn't do it. It had to be approved. We were about two years in at this point, and we were approaching some important crossroads involving worship, staffing, and a few other key areas of our branding. I knew we would never get past these intersections under our current "discuss, debate, and vote" congregationally led system.

Re-focus your priorities in the midst of daily challenges. Watch "Clarity of the Call" at **www.nlpg.com/bnc.**

Discover the difference between an invitation and God's call for our lives, and how this powerful principle guides you in keeping the daily struggles in perspective.

So I went to the deacons and said, "Hey, what if we develop a team of individuals to research the constitution and bylaws of the church and see what we would need to change to allow us to work most efficiently and (most importantly) most biblically?" They were like, "That would be awesome!" (In all honesty, they didn't even know what the current constitution said, and in all honesty, I didn't let on where I knew this process would take us.) They let me pick my own research team, and I chose five men that I knew were of like mind who would be willing to let God's Word speak for itself. We started researching bylaws and biblically based constitutions from churches of every size from every denomination. Some churches had 1 page of bylaws and some had 50. We looked most seriously at the structures of some of the fastest-growing congregations in the country, and in less than two months, we came up with about seven pages of our own.[1] Some of the key elements:

---

1. Feel free to download a copy of our constitution and bylaws at brandnewchurch.com. And if you're up for it, feel free to join the discussion on the forum attached to that site. Deciding to get the right structure, I believe, is one of the four most important decisions that a rural pastor must make. If we can help you along that process in any way, we would love to.

We changed the title "deacon" to "servant leader" (*deaconos*). In our neck of the woods and too often in other places, people think "deacon" means "I am in charge." That isn't what it means; it means "I am a servant."

We added a "trustee team." There are no biblical requirements on that one. We say you just have to love God and have a passion for your church. No distinction between female or male; we just need people in there who can help us that have a loyalty to the vision and enough passion for God to get on board with it.

Then we created an "elder board," the *episkopos,* which makes up our staff. They are the leaders of the church — the decision makers who vote on just four things: (1) the calling of the senior pastor, (2) the buying or selling of any real estate, (3) the election of trustees, and (4) the yearly budget.

We proposed the new bylaws on February 11, 2005. According to *Robert's Rules of Order,* we tabled them for a month to give everyone a chance to take a good look. They didn't. The night before the next meeting a few people started reading it and I started getting calls saying, "Hey, whoa, whoa, whoa! It looks like you are getting too much power."

The next night at the meeting, I did my best to explain. I said, "It isn't about power; it is about accurate structure." We talked Bible for a bit then I gave some illustrations. "Most rural pastors may hear from God but they can't go forward because someone else is leading the church other than them. Listen, a pilot needs to be able to fly the airplane. If he needs to push the throttles up to make it over the next mountain range, does he go back and take a vote from the passengers? You're telling me you trust me with your kids' salvation, with marrying your grandkids, with baptizing your wife . . . but you don't trust me enough to lead in the way we are going to go? If a doctor is doing a surgery and there are complications, he needs to be able to fix it right there on the spot. What does he do, go out and take a poll and say, 'Um, excuse me, this guy is hemorrhaging pretty bad. I think it'll take about an extra $4,134.99 to stop the bleeding. All in favor say, "Aye." Opposed? Same sign'."

The discussion that day was lively but civil. There was plenty of disagreement. The whole proposal would likely have been stonewalled if people had read the bylaws earlier. I'm sure, given the chance, they would have mobilized their opposition more aggressively. But it didn't happen; they didn't have the time. Still, that day was our first time during our tenure at the church to have no votes; but there weren't enough to stop the change. We had done it. In 90 days we radically changed the way things had been done for more than 50 years.

At the same time, other important factors were also coming together: the new campus, the new youth initiative, some progressive innovations in our worship — everything began to synergize under this new leadership structure, and all of a sudden everything took off. The new, biblical framework was the launching pad that took us to the next level.

Flying High, Crashing Hard

We had less than 30 days to fix up the new church building. By default we called it the "South Campus," and it needed a ton of work. We dressed it up aesthetically as best we could, and we had our first service in it March 30, 2005. The logistics were crazy, but it worked! We staggered the schedules and alternated the worship service and Sunday school times so I could blitz between the two buildings. We had been averaging about 190 at the North Campus, but that first week we packed out the South Campus, too, effectively growing from 200 to 300 overnight. It was transformed life after transformed life. I was totally jazzed.

We did the first major Wednesday youth night about the same time. It was just like the old days in Oklahoma: crazy fun, loud music, and a soul-searching message. When we counted heads, we came up with 81 kids who were literally jumping the pews that evening (you know where this is headed, don't you?) — 81 kids: 21 more than required by the vote the month before that said the pews with the plaques could be removed. I thought that was all settled, so we started ordering chairs. We had $50,000 in the fund for the building we were going to build, so we ordered some nice chairs that would come in a couple months and then ran off to the nearest Lowes to get a pile of temporary plastic ones.

When we started unscrewing pews, there was an eruption of anger on a scale of which I could have never imagined. Bruce had called charter members of the congregation to let them know what was going on. (Sensitive as I was, I thought some of them might want a pew for their home or farm — kind of a keepsake from decades past.) He took the first wave of fury over the phone, and then they descended on him at the church. He's a bulldog, and he squared off with them face to face. I had never heard of anything like it in my life: three or four families yelling and screaming and crying about their mother or grandfather. (I don't know why people blame everything on their dead relatives, but man, they were going for it.)

When I caught news of it, I was stunned. I tried to tell them they were welcome to take the pews with their memorialized plaques, or we could take the plaques off for them. Bruce pulled out the minutes to the last meeting and said, "Listen, you voted for this!" I tried to smooth things over, but the damage was already done. They responded as if I had dug up Grandpa's grave and spit on his casket. *Dang! What is it with this memorial thing?* We even had a little clock in the church that probably cost seven dollars; it had its own plaque reading "In loving memory of so-and-so." *What happens if I move that thing?*

It felt like our *Titanic* had hit the iceberg. Just when we thought we were getting to the bottom of the issue, the pews turned out to be just the tip. I was soon to find out that frustration and dissension floated far, far beneath the surface. The congregation would vote yes and smile to my face, then badmouth the decision outside the meeting. Change was coming hard, our progress was screwing with their past, and resentment was running very, very deep — which is no surprise now, but it was a shock to me then. After all, this was my first pastorate; I thought everyone was on board; I thought everyone's smiles and nods told the truth. I also thought I wanted to be the top dog, but then I found out that the one in the lead is the one with the target painted on his back. (No more hiding behind foosball tables!)

The next Sunday, you would have thought the devil was at the South Lead Hill campus, and I was the devil. Three or four families showed up. Some of the families had already left, never to return. Some returned for a while, probably thinking, *Okay, it is not over yet; we can still run him off.* I began to realize that they hired me thinking they wanted change, but they really didn't. They wanted to be engaged to change and stay married to their traditions. Such tradition requires a trade — a swapping of fresh ideas and progress for the certainty and control of the status quo. I began to realize that many struggling rural churches don't want a real pastor to lead them; they just want a pacifier to nurse them through the years.

The mass exodus from South Lead Hill was the hardest thing I had ever experienced in my life — the first real cut of rejection, the shedding of the first drops of the blood of failure. I went home and bawled. Disillusioned, defensive, wounded, I was ready to pack up and head out. Many churches were still calling me about a pastor position, some really, really nice ones offering great pay, cars, and housing allowances . . . and always willing to pay our moving expenses. I still believed that rural America was the greatest mission on earth, but during that season I was not at all sure I wanted to pay the price to be used to reach it. I would be crying in my office when someone would call and tell me that I had robbed their family, I had stolen their life. One family actually accused me of killing their mother. She died shortly after the pew incident, and they were insistent that the stress I had caused was the reason. Then I'd go home and listen to a string of dirty, accusatory messages on the phone. *Is this really worth it?* I thought.

I share what I learned from these challenges in "Prepare to Lead" at **www.nlpg.com/ bnc.**

It is vital that you be ready to make the hard decisions to fulfill God's call, which also make you a target for those who do not support your vision.

I stood on the fence, not knowing whether to stay and fight or shake the dust from my feet and walk. But I was also learning — learning valuable lessons, learning what they never tell you about rural ministry:

. . . and I was never told that, as a rural pastor, I was going to be hated. And as a hated man, I was never told that Vision, Attitude, Leadership, Understanding, and Enduring Excellence would be necessary not only to thrive but just to survive.

What They Never Told Me about Rural Ministry

- ✐ It was the most difficult job on earth.
- ✐ Friends would become enemies.
- ✐ That the people who left my church were going to be glaring at me in the check-out lane of Wal-Mart for the rest of my life.
- ✐ I was going to be thrown in the pit.
- ✐ A red-hot marriage was a must for being an effective rural pastor.
- ✐ Scripture never gives us qualifications for the office, but it gives us tons of Scriptures for the home.

Tears flowed like spring creeks during that season. It seemed like the end of the road, but the journey had really just begun.

transforming church *in* RURAL AMERICA

breaking all the RURALS

PART 2

V.A.L.U.E.

For nothing is impossible with God (Luke 1:37).

4
VISION

Vision:
When Seeing Requires Believing

[Jesus said,] "Everything is possible for him who believes."
Immediately the boy's father exclaimed, "I do believe; help
me overcome my unbelief!" (Mark 9:23–24).

Vision — I've never met a shepherd or a rancher or a farmer
who didn't have it. Sure, they might not be able to verbalize it,
but they get it; they understand it. They always have. Unlike so
much of American Christianity, which talks about it all the time
but rarely does anything about it, those who make a living from
the land understand the foundations; they know the principles.
And day by day, season by season, year after year, they live their

lives accordingly. Yes, rural Americans understand vision, and they understand belief.

I have never met a rancher who expects his herd to grow and multiply without a lot of hard work and without a lot of strategic effort. I have never met a farmer who expects a harvest without first working the soil, planting the seed, and praying for rain. They care for the land that they have, and then strategically expand their fields so the harvest might increase. They know inherently that unless things reproduce and the cycle of life is nurtured so that it can repeat itself over and over again, everything will eventually die. They are truly brilliant; they understand and apply the most powerful principles of life. Vision and belief is bred into the DNA of a rural community, and they take that wisdom with them everywhere they go . . . until, it seems, they step in the door of the church.

Too many rural pastors I know have little vision, if any. Very few have a call, if any. They don't have a vision for what they want their staff to look like, so their staffs do not operate correctly. They don't have a vision for what the building needs to look like, so it falls into archaic disrepair. They don't have a vision for their marriage, so love and passion slowly fade. They don't have a vision for their personal worship, so they fall into complacency. I am learning some are content with a "small" everything — except a small paycheck.

Add to that committees and boards that are paralyzed with indecision, bogged down with bureaucracy, and shackled by tradition. I believe it's the greatest pitfall of the rural church (and probably most American churches in general): *they have no vision.* I've even had a three-decade Christ follower say, "Well, what is a vision anyway?" I'm telling you, if rural Americans ran their farms and ranches the way most of them run their churches, the whole country would starve in short order.

I firmly believe that the five most important goals for a rural church are the following:

VALUE

V ision
A ttitude
L eadership
U nderstanding
E nduring Excellence

Each one of these V.A.L.U.E.s is indispensable — you're just not going to make it without all of them. However, I believe that vision is primary, because vision drives everything. What is vision?

Vision Is the Desired: Vision can be understood in the mind, but it's something that must be felt in the gut. It is the ability to see something that *is not*, yet it is so compelling that we know it is something that *must be,* and something that, by God's grace, *will be.*

Vision Is the Direction: Vision shows you where you are, reveals where God wants you to be, and lights the road to get there. But it doesn't mean He is going to give you the car. Vision is going wherever God calls us to go and then finding or creating the vehicle to get us there, by a sovereign mixture of God's provision and our exertion.

Vision Is Defining: Vision is not illusion. It brings focus and practicality to everything we do. With clear vision, everything you and I embark on can, and must, be in line with the overall vision of your church. As such, vision defines everything we are and everything we do. The vision of our church is to **Worship Him, Walk with Him, and Welcome Others to Him.** Every event, every decision, every sermon — *everything* — is defined by that vision. And if it doesn't fit, it gets scrapped. Within that vision we focus on four non-negotiables: the Weekend Experience, Children/Student Ministry, Volunteers, and Community Groups. If you do not have defined vision for your church, the loudest member will define it for you.

Vision Is Dynamic: Vision is us in action, hearing what God wants us to do then providing the vehicle to allow that vision to come to fruition. I'm not talking about motion but a movement. There is a big difference. I'm not talking about activity, I'm talking about focused strategic action — and those actions, strategies, and focuses are dynamic as well. Today's innovations will become the traditions of tomorrow, and all of those need to be negotiable as circumstances change and we do whatever it takes to fulfill the unchanging vision God has given us.

Vision Is in the Deity: Vision comes from God, and vision belongs to God — not us. When I was growing up, I would turn on the TV and see Adrian Rogers, or read a book by Charles Stanley and see a picture on the back cover of an unbelievable church campus. I remember driving through Memphis and seeing the magnificent facilities of Bellevue Baptist Church. I thought it was awesome that these places were available to their communities, and I still do.

The problem was that I adopted their vision as my own vision. It was a painful day when I came to the realization that my vision of my ministry was not God's vision. When I let go of my personal vision, there was room for God's vision to begin. And it grew and is growing, expanding beyond anything I could have imagined.

God-Driven Vision: Yes, "vision is the desired," but it must be God's desire, not ours. That requires unqualified surrender and submission to Him. God is the one who drives our vision, and He is the one who drives our life. (Ditch the "God is my co-pilot" bumper sticker — that is imprecise and unbiblical.)

I recently read Francis Chan's book *Crazy Love,* and some questions he asked have been ringing through my head. Do you agree with any of the following?

Are the Following True of You?

- You passionately love Jesus, but you don't really want to be like Him.

- You admire His humility, but you don't want to be THAT humble.

- You think it's beautiful that He washed the feet of the disciples, but that's not exactly the direction your life is headed.

- You're thankful He was spit upon and abused, but you would never let that happen to you.

- You praise Him for loving you enough to suffer during His whole time on earth, but you're going to do everything within your power to make sure you enjoy your time down here.

In short: you think He's a great Savior, but not a great role model. In 1 John 2:6 it says, "Whoever claims to live in him must walk as Jesus did." The American church has abandoned the most simple and obvious truth of what it means to follow Jesus: you actually follow His pattern of life. You should not just love Jesus; you need to look like Jesus.

We need to stop and think about that. Let's make a personal decision to stop talking so much and begin living like Jesus. Our personal visions must be released before God's visions can be embraced. I'm making no apologies for how difficult and how necessary that is. Our personal dreams, desires, and visions die painfully hard. But die they must. (And then we find that they have this amazing capacity to resurrect themselves time and time again.)

God's vision for your church may not look like the current, trendy church down the road or the latest success story you hear about at a conference. We are so apt to do what someone else has done instead of declaring God's vision for each of us. Divine vision is not borrowed from someone else and is not imposed by someone else. Vision must come from Him through you, and that requires submission on your part and the willingness to follow Him regardless of what you want, regardless of what your denomination wants, no matter what your dad or spouse expects, regardless of what the accountants on your finance committee say is responsible. Is it possible to embrace God-driven vision in all circumstances? Yes. Yes, it is. God can do this through you. Perhaps the Apostle Paul said it best:

> I know what it is to be in need, and I know what it is to have plenty. I have learned the secret of being content in any and every situation, whether well fed or hungry, whether living in plenty or in want. I can do everything through him who gives me strength (Phil. 4:12–13).

God-Dependent Vision: *I can do everything through Him who gives me strength.* Do you believe that? We will talk more about the importance of your belief in a moment, but just know that one of the tests of a God-driven vision is that it can only be accomplished if God does it. Your own vision will likely be something you can plan or orchestrate and do on your own.

In rural settings we see floundering fellowships, dispersing congregations, and decaying small buildings. We see facilities struggling with small budgets and limited ministry potential. But a God-driven, God-dependent vision allows you to see with faith eyes, not just facts. We'll see that we don't need renovations, we need miracles. We need to step out in a way that reflects total and bold dependence on God's leading in God's provision. But remember, just because the vision is outlandish doesn't mean that it came from God. But I believe the true God-driven vision is far enough "out there" that it requires God-dependence. If not, your soul is missing out on making right decisions, on going forward, and on doing the things that make a supernatural difference. And this brings us to a critical and important intersection. Because in order to have vision from God, and in order to pursue it, we have to believe. . . and I mean *really* believe.

This We Believe!

As Christians, we believe some truly amazing things. Your church's belief statements may be gathering dust in the back of a file cabinet in the secretary's office, or they may be as commonplace and as rote as the Pledge of Allegiance being recited by a third grader. No matter, let's dust them off or speak of them as if they are brand new for a few moments, because what we truly believe changes everything.

Foundational Christian Beliefs

God created the world — Genesis 1:1:
In the beginning God created the heavens and the earth.

God scripted the Holy Word of God — 2 Timothy 3:16:
All Scripture is God-breathed. . . .

Jesus Christ was born of a virgin — Matthew 1:23:
The virgin will be with child and will give birth to a son, and they will call him Immanuel.

Jesus is the sinless Son of God — Hebrews 4:15:
For we do not have a high priest who is unable to sympathize with our weaknesses, but we have one who has been tempted in every way, just as we are — yet was without sin.

Salvation is real and found only through Jesus Christ — Acts 4:12:
Salvation is found in no one else, for there is no other name under heaven given to men by which we must be saved.

Jesus rose from the dead — Acts 10:41:
He was not seen by all the people, but by witnesses whom God had already chosen — by us who ate and drank with him after he rose from the dead.

These are *monster* beliefs. I mean, take another look at those things. No wonder the non-believing world thinks that the Church is absolutely crazy. *How can they believe God inspired and compiled the Bible? How can they believe that Jesus Christ was born of a virgin? I mean, come on!* Yet, as "believers" we meet together each week, gathering because these truths have moved us to obedience, because we believe.

Or Do We?

I'm asking that honestly. If we really believed, wouldn't we really be stepping out as if these things were true? Why do we too often have this huge theological faith, Christological faith, bibliological faith, creation faith, soteriological faith . . . *and then display such a midget, powerless God working within our church and our lives?* By God's grace, most of us would die for what we say we believe. With a gun to our heads we would probably take a bullet rather than deny Christ as our Lord and God the Father as the all-powerful, all-knowing, sovereign One of the universe. But I'm asking you, if that's what we believe, why don't we believe God for the day-to-day stuff, when it comes to the back-pocket issues of our lives?

This is critical, because without belief we will step right up to the edge of God-driven, God-dependent vision . . . and then back away in fear, hiding behind pious, corporate doubt. Pastors, leaders, and church volunteers often struggle to believe:

- that God can remove the church bully;

- that God can ignite a spiritual fire and revival within the "church family";

- that God can provide the resources for faith-filled ministries;

- that God can use your church to reach the world;

⌒ that God can change the way it's always been;

⌒ that God cares about my church;

⌒ that God can use me to change my rural community.

When we look at the challenges, and then we look at ourselves, who are we to think that God can use us to make a difference? Listen, I know what you're talking about. I feel it every day. But if we give in to those feelings, we're going to miss one of the most liberating truths of our faith: vision is realized not because of us but because of the God who uses us. Consider the kinds of people God has hired onto His staff team over the centuries from this very familiar list:

Noah was a drunk (Gen. 9:21).
Jacob was a liar (Gen. 27).
Leah was ugly (Gen. 29:16–18).
Joseph was abused (Gen. 37:22–28).
Moses had a stuttering problem (Exod. 4:10).
Gideon was afraid (Judg. 6:15).
Samson had long hair and was a womanizer
    (Judg. 16:5–17).
Rahab was a harlot (Josh. 2:1).
Jeremiah and Timothy were too young
    (Jer. 1:6).
David had an affair and was a murderer
    (2 Sam. 11:2–4 and 14–17).
Elijah was suicidal (1 Kings 19:4).
Isaiah preached naked (Isa. 20:2).
Jonah ran from God (Jon. 1:3).
Naomi was a widow (Ruth 1:3).
Job went bankrupt (Job 1:21).
Peter denied Christ (Mark 14:71).
The disciples fell asleep while praying (Matt. 26:40).
Martha worried about everything (Luke 10:40–42).
The Samaritan woman was divorced, more than once
    (John 4:17–18).
Zaccheus was too small (Luke 19:2–3).

Paul was too religious (Acts 22:1–5).
Timothy had an ulcer (1 Tim. 5:23).
Lazarus was dead (John 11).

These are not exactly cream-puff seminary grads. How could God use them? How can He use us? My wife Cindy was once asked, "How come you and Shannon are so lovey toward each other . . . holding hands, kisses and hugs so often?" Cindy's response was simply "Jesus Christ in us." If you are having a hard time believing that God can use you, and if you ask me why I believe that He can, I'll give you the same simple response: "Jesus Christ in you."

"Christ in you" is not lofty theology; it is powerful reality. Paul proclaimed, "I have been crucified with Christ and I no longer live, but Christ lives in me. The life I live in the body, I live by faith in the Son of God" (Gal. 2:20). Left to ourselves, we would absolutely be toast. Asking God to "help us" in our weaknesses is a step in the right direction but doesn't grasp the full implications of the fact that all of God's power resides within. He resides in you so that you can take His vision and let Him make it a reality through you. He has geared and wired you, and now He lives in you so that He can further His vision for His church. God does it; He provides it, but don't think that vision is just something that is going to happen. For some reason, He has chosen to use human beings to glorify Himself; as His vessels we enable God's vision. That is why we are here; that is why the Spirit of God lives within us.

Bringing it to Our Knees

I believe God wants me to pray for the Body of Christ. In particular, He has given me one overarching prayer for the Church. It's found in John 3:16, *"For God so loved the world, that he gave his one and only Son, that whoever believes. . . ."* My prayer is that He would make us believe. My prayer is that the Church, the Body of Christ, our congregations spread out across rural and metro America, would take the Bible and not just listen to it, but *believe* it — really believe it. MAKE US BELIEVE! Because when the Church does not believe, when the "us" (the Church) is removed, guess what? It's just MAKE BELIEVE. See, many of us believe *in* Christ. We recite the Apostles' Creed or Nicene Creed and confess that we believe in Him. But many of us have not jumped the hurdle of believing Christ. We believe in Him theologically (mentally), but we don't believe Him practically.

My prayer is "God, make us believe!" Because when you say, "I believe Jesus," you go to the next level in your walk with Him. When the Church, the Body of Christ, says, "We believe Jesus," then the whole congregation goes to the next level and they further "the vision."

My prayer is "God, make us believe!" It's no wonder the unbelieving world thinks Christianity is make believe. They're asking themselves the question: *Where is the Church?* I'll tell you where we are — we are in some committee meeting, trying to figure out what color the bathrooms should be painted, rather than pursuing, seeking, and living supernatural vision through the power of Christ who lives in us.

My prayer is "God, make us believe!" Let truth be real. Be real in our lives. Without belief, we cannot have vision. Unless we believe Jesus, we will never see beyond what is; we will never dream of what could be beyond what we see. Because of that, I'm compelled to pray that four statements made by Christ become real, really real to us — that our vision might be ignited according to the truth about who God is and who we are in Him. I'm praying that we wouldn't just believe in Him but that we would take Him at His Word and believe Him, period.

I pray that God will make us believe Jesus, who said, "All things are possible."

Now that is a sweet-sounding bookmark, but I want us, I want the Body of Christ (beginning with me!) to believe *all* things are *possible*. If you look up the word *all* in the original Greek and study its etymology, you'll find it means this: "all." Jesus said, "All things are possible," but the tragedy is that the Church is not believing it. We take out the "all" and insert "some." Most of us can't envision anything outside of what seems prudent and practical. As a result, we are doing everything possible and nothing impossible. We do what seems logical — things that the Church can do in its own strength, things in our comfort zones, things that our budget can handle. I pray God will make us believe Jesus, who said: *"With man this is impossible, but with God all things are possible"* (Matt. 19:26).

> I tell you the truth, if you have faith as small as a mustard seed, you can say to this mountain, "Move from here to there" and it will move. Nothing will be impossible for you (Matt. 17:20).

> *I am begging God to make us believe Jesus, who said, "Ask and you will receive."*

I'm not talking about praying to win *American Idol* or praying for a million dollars on the end of your bed — let's not even go there. On the other hand, I'm also not talking about the milquetoast prayers of most local churches that are little more than cop-outs. So many are afraid to ask boldly because, "Well, it may not be God's will." We need to get past that. Listen, if you are praying according to God's Word, you are praying according to His will. So I'm praying that we will get in His Word so we can boldly pray according to His will, in His name, guaranteeing that our prayers will be heard. I am begging God to make us believe Jesus, who said:

> Until now, you have not asked for anything in my name. Ask and you will receive, and your joy will be complete (John 16:24).

I'm pleading with God to make us believe Jesus, who said, "You will do even greater things than these."

Think of some of the things Jesus did. He fed the 5,000. He turned the water into wine. He healed many people. He fed thousands that were desperate and listening to His message. Now, the Spirit of God has come into our hearts. Though we struggle with sin and the flesh, we have that same ability, the same power of God living within us that Jesus did.

Here's my problem. Our arithmetic is failing. We have a "less than" mentality rather than a "greater than" mentality — and we aren't even comparing ourselves to Christ, we are comparing ourselves to the status quo. We are settling for the same size, the same stuff, the same approach. The same, the same, the same . . . Jesus said we would not only do far more than that; He said we would do more than He did! So I'm pleading with God to make us believe Jesus, who said,

I tell you the truth, anyone who has faith in me will do what I have been doing. He will do even greater things than these (John 14:12).

Finally, I am wholeheartedly beseeching God to make us believe Jesus, who said, "I am coming soon."

I'm afraid that we may have lost this expectation altogether. It's one of those truths that we might take a peek at every once in a while on a Sunday morning, and then we go about the rest of our 24/7 without any urgency, without any sort of vision. If the world events of the last decade have taught us anything, it should be this: history as we know it will not and cannot continue on indefinitely. The world is on a course with destiny. In the blink of an eye Christ will return just as He has promised. Yet few of us have ever really contemplated how the implications of that future event should be affecting our lives today, because, in all honesty, I'm not sure we truly believe it. So finally, I am wholeheartedly beseeching God to make us believe Jesus, who said:

Behold, I am coming soon! My reward is with me, and
I will give to everyone according to what he has done
(Rev. 22:12).

Imagine

Can you imagine, can you fathom, can you grasp what
would happen if you, if we, if the whole Church really believed
Christ and these four simple statements He made? What if we
really believe that all things were possible? How big might we
dream? Could God free us from our addictions? Could He heal
our marriages? Could He bring life into our families, into our
workplaces, into our neighborhoods? How far out of the box
might God take us with His visions and His possibilities?

What if we really began to ask, praying fervently according
to His will as it is revealed in Scripture? What if we aligned our
hearts with what was true and seriously begged God to make
that truth a reality in our lives and the lives around us? Imagine,
if we asked these things in His name, how complete might our
joy actually be.

Imagine if we really believed that we could do the things
that Christ did, and even do greater things than He did! How
would that affect our vision? What would be the possibilities?
Already He has given us technology to do things that no one
could have ever, ever dreamed of in the days Jesus walked on
this earth. And finally, can you imagine how invigorated and
empowered we would be as individuals and as a Body if we
truly came to believe that our time on this earth might be
very, very short, that Jesus Himself is coming back to claim all
history for Himself? Don't you think that we would be serious
(not about programs, and not about conferences, and not about
another big cantata), but we would be serious about reaching
the lost? Doing whatever it takes, as His Body, to reach them ...
because He's coming back!

My prayer is "God, make us believe!" If only we believed the things that He has already told us are true. What freedom we would have as we laid down our own dreams and allowed Christ to work through us as He sees fit for His glory. We would be transformed — the world would be changed, turned upside-down by believers and churches that were finally able to dream dreams and receive the vision of God's calling in their personal and corporate lives.

My prayer is "God, make us believe!" The world is desperate to see us living it — the real deal, the transformation only Jesus can make in our lives. MAKE US BELIEVE. Otherwise, it'll just be MAKE BELIEVE and the world will say, "Oh, I've seen that before." "I know what goes on at a church." "I know typical church." There are people, associates, family members, parents that are literally dying to see a difference. If we believe, they will see the real deal.

Here in rural America we are faithful and hard-working people. We have vision and we have belief in the other areas of our lives. We till the soil, we plant the seed, we pray for rain and work in the harvest — and we are thankful for the miracle of it all when things grow and multiply. Now we need to bring those attributes into the Church. We have for too long put our hope in the next conference, the next "great" message, the next big donation (which I do not oppose!). But these things have, in too many cases, taken the place of the Holy God of the universe, the King of kings, the Maker of heaven and earth to power the mighty vision He has given us.

I'm ready to believe. I no longer want to settle. I no longer want to just live life. I want to believe that all things are possible, that my loved one can be rescued by His power. That my finances can change. That my influence on my campus can change. That my marriage can change. That my church can grow and explode in the area God's called me to.

I wrestle with belief just like you. My personal prayers to Jesus echo the pleas of the desperate father who brought his tormented son to Christ:

"If you can do anything, take pity on us and help us." . . . "Everything is possible for him who believes," Jesus replied. Immediately the boy's father exclaimed, "I do believe; help me overcome my unbelief!" (Mark 9:22–24)

I believe that God still answers that request today. *I believe. Help my unbelief.* And if you will just get honest with God and cry out to Him, His vision will be made plain to you. He has gifted and geared and wired you and put you where you are geographically for a purpose, and the power of His Spirit resides in your spirit, ready to make His purposes become a reality. This world is starving for people with vision, so I pray that God will make us believe!

I pray also that the eyes of your heart may be enlightened in order that you may know the hope to which he has called you, the riches of his glorious inheritance in the saints, and his incomparably great power for us who believe (Eph. 1:18–19).

Visit Shannon's blog to keep track of the latest BNC news, insights on rural leadership, and strategies on engaging your community.

My prayer is for vision and real belief among the leadership of the rural church. I believe this is the heart of the battle for all believers. At www.BreakingAllTheRurals.com we are reaching out a prayer for the worldwide Church. Proclaim the vision God is giving you so that together we can pray in agreement for His will to be done. We invite you to be a part of an effort to make our requests known to God and to stand together in these difficult times, and overcome the doubt that dilutes belief.

5
ATTITUDE

Sacred Cows and Slaughtering the Status Quo

> Your attitude should be the same as that of Christ Jesus: who, being in very nature God, did not consider equality with God something to be grasped, but made himself nothing, taking the very nature of a servant, being made in human likeness. And being found in appearance as a man, he humbled himself and became obedient to death — even death on a cross! (Phil. 2:5–8).

Everyone likes change — except when it makes things different. Let's be honest; human beings are kind of weird that way. (We are weird in a lot of ways, but let's not go there right now. . . .)

Four Things We Want

1   Progress, but not the unknown that comes with it.

2   Security and stability, but not the stagnation.

3   Love, but not at the risk of rejection.

4   Adventure, but not the unpredictable journey of charting a new course.

What we *want* is yesterday, today, and tomorrow all tied up in one neat little package — a package that does not exist. What we *need* is a well-honed attitude emerging from a disciplined mind and a faithful heart. This is one of the most difficult — and yet important — junctions we face on the journey through rural ministry, and it must be navigated correctly. If your ministry is going to reflect VALUE, you must have not only vision, you must have attitude. As Paul exhorts us in Philippians chapter 2, *your attitude should be the same as that of Christ Jesus.* This attitude contains energy, purpose, realistic optimism, and the willingness to make self-sacrifice for the cause. Nothing depletes the effectiveness of your vision more than a bad attitude. Nothing energizes it like attitude that is modeled after Christ and empowered by Christ, who lives in us. You want VALUE? Then simply make sure all leaders, volunteers, staff, and events are filled with this attitude and energy.

Easier said than done.

Black Sunday Revisited

I have to admit, the "Battle of the Pews" blindsided me. Looking back, I can't believe I didn't see it coming, but I really didn't. I naïvely thought that everyone in the congregation really wanted to change. Why else would they have hired somebody as nuts as me? But I found out the hard way that what people *say* they want, what they *think* they want, and what they actually really *do* want can be totally different things. That day I learned that people say they want to reach the lost, until we start changing things they are familiar and comfortable with in order to do what it takes to really reach the lost. When we crashed into the sacred-cow pews, our congregation had a true "collision of vision" that revealed the differences in how we truly looked at change . . . and it felt like a train crash.

In an emergency situation like that, when we as rural pastors are looking around at all the wreckage, sincere questions must be answered:

> ### Questions to Ask in a Crisis
>
> Do we fight or do we back down?
>
> Do we stay or do we leave?
>
> Is it time for compromise or do we hold fast?

Ultimately, however, we have to answer the question *Am I called or not?* If the answer is yes, then we need to dig a little bit deeper: *is my vision tied to this venue or is it time to go somewhere else?* If you realize that your call is to a community and not necessarily to a congregation, it might be a viable option to start over with a brand-new church in the same area. Unless you have a clear call from God, moving on in one form or another is truly an option. I find that a lot of pastors are staying for the wrong reasons. It might be the fear of losing their paycheck (small as it may be); it might be the expectations of other people (including a spouse or kids who like where they are); it might be a vocational fear (gosh, what else would I do? If I'm not a pastor, who am I?); and it might just be a simple fear of change in and of itself.

Are you really called to rural America? If you are, you better pony up because it is going to be the greatest opportunity and also the biggest challenge you have ever experienced, particularly when people leave, because even though they leave the church, they are never, ever gone from your life. The people that leave your church today will be pumping gas next to you tomorrow, and the next day they will be shopping on row 12 at Wal-Mart just like you, because there is only one Wal-Mart in your whole county. You will share the bleachers at every game and see them at every community outing. In a small town you will be running into that family — that person who left, that person who never wanted you as part of the church — over and over and over again for years if you stick around.

The county we serve in is one of the largest counties in the state of Arkansas as far as land mass goes, yet it has a population of approximately 25,000 people. There's lots of wide-open space, but it still is impossible to avoid people you don't want to see. Are you called to rural America? If you are, you better get some tough skin. You have got to find out: am I *really* called to this gig? If you are, you better be ready to beg God to show up because there is nothing sexy and there are no frills and there is no money . . . and you are stuck with these people.

Am I really called to the sticks? You need to have that question answered before the tough times set in and you have to figure out what to do next. Me? I had no choice but to stay. I knew that *this* church was my call from God, and I was ready to fight the battle until new orders came in. (So far, they haven't.) Your call should be approached as a call to marriage or you will be in the lawyer's office at the first sign of irreconcilable differences. But in all honesty, I wasn't looking for a way out. Even though it hurt, it didn't dent my passion or smear my vision. God had placed the rurals on my heart. This is where I wanted to be, truly. I couldn't and didn't want to change that. What needed to change, however, was my attitude.

Essential Attitude

Philippians 2 is packed with powerful, profound, even mystical truth about the reality of who Jesus Christ is and what He did. Christ, who is fully God — eternal and unchanging — changed. Without compromising who He is, He made Himself nothing, transformed into human likeness and morphed into a servant. The miracle of "Emmanuel" was laid bare for all to see that first Christmas as He changed — truly changed — so that He could become obedient to His call, even obedience to the point of death on the Cross.

Powerful. And that's the attitude that the apostle Paul says we are to have as well. Such an attitude involves a willingness to not only embrace things that are new, but to also stop doing things that are old and familiar. Yes, we need to be willing to start, but we need to be willing to stop. I'll admit it took a long time to understand and be comfortable with that. It has been one of many things I have learned the hard way. But at least I'm not alone. Scripture is full of stop signs:

- Job 37:14:
  Listen to this, Job; stop and consider God's wonders.
- Isaiah 1:16:
  Stop doing wrong.
- Amos 7:5:
  Then I cried out, "Sovereign Lord, I beg you, stop!"
- Luke 8:52:
  "Stop wailing," Jesus said.
- John 5:14:
  Stop sinning or something worse may happen to you.
- Romans 14:13:
  Therefore let us stop passing judgment on one another.

- 1 Corinthians 14:20:
  Brothers, stop thinking like children.

I even created my first "Stop Doing List," which includes the following:

- Focusing only on what needs to be tweaked and not celebrating the peaks.
- Being opposed through pride and start receiving grace through humility.
- Thinking people who are not with me are against me.
- Stop believing I have to do it all.

As a leader, learning from mistakes is the key to success — and I have made a ton. These are not in any order but are definite no-no's for the remaining days of my life and ministry:

TEN THINGS I'D NEVER DO AGAIN

10   Ask my wife when we are arguing, "Have you had your quiet time with God today?"

9   Believe ministry success is based on the size of your congregation.

8   Miss a date night with Cindy!

7   Say yes to everything.

6   Believe everything people tell me.

5   Believe it is God's will for everyone who joins the church but not His will for everyone who leaves.

4   Listen to the advice of those who have never taken a spiritual risk of faith in ministry.

3   Preach a prayer-less message.

2   Believe that God needs me.

1   Take a job for the salary and benefit package.

It's much easier to stop doing something negative if we have a positive thing to take its place. While churches get excited about personal change and transformation, there can be stubborn resistance to change when it comes to the facility itself. Vision can help but not cure this.

When we first got to Southside, we had an entryway cover at the old church that was about as wide as my shoulders; it was about the size of a cardboard television box — with even less aesthetic value. It was silly that it was even hanging there — kind of an eave, but not really. I took it to the board and said, "Hey, let's change that." The first thing they said was, "We don't have the money to do it." (But at least that thing didn't have a memorial plaque on it.) To get rid of that thing was going to require subcommittees and budget amendments, and I'm thinking, *This will never get done.* So Cindy and I paid for it and had it done in a week. Well, the people of Southside had never heard of that being done before. Nothing had ever been done that way before. They were stunned. Anything that happened in that church needed to be debated, discussed, and voted on. They *said* the problem was that they didn't have the money, but when we took that excuse away, the issue of control and change was revealed. In the past, the sheep had dictated every step the shepherd was able to take. But we took that one step on our own, and nobody died.

About a year and a half into the journey, our first big building project began to take shape. The church had grown to about 95 in a year — I mean really cool growth. Lives were being changed; people were getting baptized. It was great to see the place filling up. But when nature called, all these people had to go down two flights of stairs and down the hall to the other end of the building to get to the bathrooms. You really had to plan ahead. By the smell of things down there from time to time, I'm not sure everybody made it. The bathrooms had that patented aroma that results from combining Lysol, mold, and human byproducts with unrecycled air and then letting them ferment in the dark six days of the week.

We were determined that we had to have a bathroom upstairs. We did a budget on it and learned it was going to cost $30,000. That was our first big hurdle. Too often rural churches have the attitude that since we don't have tons of resources, nothing can change. But let me tell you it's not *what* we have but *who* we have. We have the God of the universe living within us and we don't even believe it! We trust Him for our salvation but not with the details and finances of our personal ministry? Hmmm . . . something is wrong here.

Anyway, we ran head first into the "can't be done" attitude. You would have thought we were building the Taj Mahal or something. But it wasn't just about the bucks. One of the walls was going to cover up one of the stained glass windows that let light in on the side of the building. When we presented the plans in a business meeting, someone argued, "Well, we just can't have that stained glass window covered. My grandmother helped build this church." *Oh man, not again, I thought. Why is resistance to change always blamed on dead relatives?*

The church was still operating as a democracy. Of course I was selling vision, but I knew that becoming a visionary church was going to take some time. The *Queen Mary* doesn't go from zero to 60 in six seconds. You don't turn the *Titanic* around on a dime . . . it takes some time. But at the same time, you have to keep moving in the direction of the vision, leading by example, telling the congregation over and over where you are going. See, you will be either the anchor of your ship or the engine. Do not hold it in a standstill; perpetuate momentum with the cylinders of passion, purpose, and pursuit.

This window was sensitive ground, and as with most committees, everyone tried to come up with some sort of a compromise. "What if we put a back light behind the stained glass to make it look like light was coming in? What if we move the wall, or move the window, or . . ." They were considering all kinds of possibilities to make everyone happy and minimize the change, but it was crazy, and none of the ideas facilitated the purpose behind the changes we needed to make in the first place.

Finally I stopped them. It was a pivotal moment, actually. The details of the wall in the window were insignificant compared to the precedent that would be set in the moments ahead. *Would this church be moving ahead according to what needed to happen to fulfill our vision? Or would we be forever shackled to our facilities and our past?* I cleared my throat. "We need a bathroom so people can come in, especially if they are handicapped or have small children. We will leave the stained glass, but there will be no light; it is going to be dark. All in favor?"

We voted it in, and we moved on. *Phew.* Sigh of relief.

Then God told me we needed to combine the north and south campuses and change the name of the church so we would be clearly unified. *Change the name of the church?! I was like, God, please. I just got over the pew deal; come on. Please no. No, please. Please, please. No no . . . God said, "Change it."*

When you became a Christ follower, you became brand-new according to Colossians 3:10: "You have begun to live the new life, in which you are being made new and are becoming like the One who made you" (NCV). When Christ comes into our lives, He doesn't just renovate or build Himself a little addition onto our hearts. He makes us completely new spiritually and then begins the lifelong process of renewing us outwardly to conform to this new inner nature. He was doing the same thing with our church as a body. We were embracing a brand-new nature and renewing the outward appearance of the church because of it. We finalized the decision as a staff, which at the time consisted of one paid staff and three volunteers. Bruce was volunteering, Beverly was volunteering, and we had a music guy that I was just getting ready to re-assign after being a highly effective transitional leader.

So that was it. We still did business as Southside Baptist, but in a God-directed twist of irony, the 56-year-old congregation would now be known as Brand New Church. It raised a lot of eyebrows, but it helped everyone know that this ship was moving on.

The End Game of Change

I'm addicted to life change. I can't get away from it. Some have to have their morning coffee; some have to have the newest book; some have got to have their next smoke — I have to be involved in people's lives and in watching them change. And that's such a key aspect of Christ-modeled attitude: we don't change just for the sake of change, we change for life-change. When we make changes, we are not trying to be innovative or clever, or to rock the boat for no good reason. We change to let God work through us more freely so we can be more effective tools of life transformation for the people God has called us to.

But even that can cause problems, because life change can be messy — really messy. Let's face it, there's something comfortable about being with people who are like us, who are predictable, and who only ask questions that we already know how to answer. There is safety inside the "Christian bubble" that makes it really, really easy to cut ourselves off from the unchurched and withhold the gospel from those who want it and need it.

That needs to change. Flat out, I want as many homosexuals, drug addicts, divorcees, and alcoholics as possible darkening the doors of Brand New Church, because those people want and need change. I want to associate with everything that is disassociated with the church in rural America, because I know that is when God shows up. I want to see the pregnant 17-year-old who was kicked out of her Christian school attend worship. I want the guys whose pickups rattle with the sound of empty beer cans to come one Sunday and decide to stay. I want the woman who has been going from bed to bed trying to find true love to attend and learn about the authentic love God has for her. Because when they show up, God shows up to impact their lives.

Yeah, it's messy. They don't know how to talk like Christians. They leave cigarette butts in the parking lot. They can't "turn to the Book of Haggai." They park in your parking spot and sit in your chair. Yet these are the ones who need and want the gospel.

And the rest of the pew sitters? They *say* they want to reach the lost. They *think* they want to reach the lost, but for some, they really don't. Messy people are just messy. To see their lives changed requires that we change our lives, sometimes at the most inconvenient, uncomfortable times and places.

So, in general, too often the rural church doesn't want to change, and yet we must change our lives in order to become life changers. And that leads to a fight worth fighting for.

Conflict "Resolution"

Growing means changing. If you are called to lead and you do it, you will grow and change. It is a promise from God. If you are influencing lives and those lives are changed, get ready for conflict, because change and growth almost always follow a very predictable order: Change, Conflict, and Growth. Once you go through the cycle two or three times, most rural leaders say, "Change? Umm, maybe not. I got a little bit of growth out of the last time, but I'm not sure I want to go through the middle part again!"

Let me be really, really honest: if you're going to grow, you're going to have to have conflict. And that's where conflict resolution comes in . . . but I'm not talking about resolving conflict through compromising (though God may call for that in many circumstances). What I'm saying is that we need to be resolved to conflict. We need to say, "Change causes growth and conflict. I take on the attitude of Jesus Christ, who fulfilled His vision by humbling Himself and serving the church even at great personal sacrifice."

As far too many soldiers have shown us, it takes great personal sacrifice to willingly enter a conflict. But if we are to fulfill our vision, we have no other choice. It's *change, conflict, growth; change, conflict, growth;* and you *have* to walk through that process. It happens on a personal level every time we see someone freed from a massive addiction. The person makes a change, then there is major conflict, but then there is unbelievable growth. It's the same with the church; we must go through change and then conflict in order to see growth. Nobody told me that before I went to rural America. But it's part of the game — one of the rules you will have to abide by play after play. When conflict comes, most rural pastors give up on change. It's just too hard. What can we do? We must be resolved to conflict in its many forms; we must pick our battles carefully, and we must choose which hills we are willing to die on — just as Jesus chose Golgotha.

When we have within ourselves the attitude of Christ, we are joining in a long legacy of self-sacrifice that Jesus Himself started. The heritage of suffering in this way was perpetuated by the early Apostles and has been part of the growing Church ever since. Take Paul for example. In Galatians 2 we find Paul returning to Jerusalem in response to a vision and revelation given by God. Like any good rural pastor, he took others with him, Barnabas and Titus. Paul is defending the gospel of liberty and freedom before those who "seem to be leaders." Initially, he was looking for their approval "for fear that I was running or had run my race in vain." At issue was the fact that Titus, who was a Gentile, had not followed in the Jewish tradition of circumcision. "This matter arose because some false brothers had infiltrated our ranks to spy on the freedom we have in Jesus Christ and to make us slaves."

Look at this — this is powerful: They were in a battle for the truth of the gospel that was being threatened by the *we've-always-done-it-this-way* message of tradition. And I'm telling you, we fight this same battle today in rural America. There are very few churches that are preaching the pure gospel of life transformation. We have this easy believism for our congregants. We have this easy believism for our leaders. They are preaching a short walk down the aisle and a prayer — but the gospel isn't an invitation to walk down an aisle and pray

— it's a call to transformation. If you will put your hands to the plow, leave everything you have and sell it all, and follow Christ, *then* you will find it. And believe me, rural Americans know what plows are about. They get this when it comes to daily life, but they're not hearing it on Sunday. Instead, they model a stagnant life of treading water and defending decades-old traditions.

The "seemed to be leaders" of this early church were defending a gospel of legalism and circumcision. Paul knew that the gospel was more than skin deep (please pardon the pun). Paul knew that the truth of the gospel reached into the soul and the spirit. Paul's gospel was freedom and liberty and watching changed lives. It wasn't based on outward appearances or adherence to old religious traditions; it was new, it was alive, and it changed things. Did they give in? Did Titus get circumcised just because that's the way it had always been done?

> Yet not even Titus, who was with me, was compelled to be circumcised, even though he was a Greek. . . . We did not give in to them for a moment, so that the truth of the gospel might remain with you (Gal. 2:3–5).

Dissolving Dynasties

Yes, conflict is the norm as the Christian takes a stand against the world, the flesh, and the devil. But particularly in rural America, fresh leaders are likely to face well-entrenched resistance and opposition from an unlikely source. Unless we recognize it for what it is, our vision can be crippled by our own "seemed to be leaders" — the families who run the rural church. Most rural churches are controlled by a handful of families. They don't represent God's family; it is a *local* family that has been running the place for 50 years. They are highly protective of the congregation and the building. Persistent tradition and generational claims on the church building are what drive them. Their vision (if you can call it that) is to control, maintain, and defend what it is, rather than pursue what could be. They will fight for their family's church more than they will fight for growing God's church. Add to this the fact that many of them are "everyday theologians" with weakly supported but strongly defended pet doctrines and you have a recipe for chaos, confusion, and ineffectiveness. These "seemed to be leaders" will appear to be your friends at first. They are hard working, punctual, supportive, and they're probably responsible for balancing the books and making sure the building doesn't collapse upon itself. They've seen plenty of pastors come and go, and they are happy to support you . . . as long as nothing is changed.

Is your organization thriving or is it just surviving? If it is just surviving, there is a great chance that you are crippled by the "seemed to be leaders" in your organization instead of getting a vision and leading through the vision. Until you take the courage and step out in obedient leadership, you will not experience the growth necessary to make a difference in your community.

It's very difficult to challenge the family dynasties that "own" most rural churches. Rural churches are in bondage. They are enslaved to the "seemed to be leaders," crippled by bureaucracy and tradition that can make true leaders fearful to make decisions and chart clear direction. We, as leaders of the rural church, are called to preach the gospel to those who are currently outside of the fold. All of the change that we implement within the church must have as its goal the transformation of lives both inside and outside of the church. We cannot let our vision become enslaved by the fear of someone who probably hasn't led anyone to Christ in decades anyway. The change will bring conflict, but following the conflict there will be growth. Paul models the way:

> As for those who seemed to be important — whatever they were makes no difference to me; God does not judge by external appearance — those men added nothing to my message. On the contrary, they saw that I had been

entrusted with the task of preaching the gospel to the Gentiles, just as Peter had been to the Jews (Gal. 2:6–7).

Please understand: it is really not about the ten families that have been there forever. It is about the families that will never experience a relevant gospel and never meet the living God unless someone with vision shows up and starts preaching the gospel with their words and with their life. Yeah, most rural churches say they want to grow, and they think they want to grow, but they really don't. They don't want a real pastor — a true and dedicated shepherd to lead them into new fields of harvest — they want somebody to pacify them, tell them what they already know, and keep things the way they are.

When you begin to live out the vision that God has given you, some of them will leave, and some of them will fight. Let's humbly and firmly engage with those who want to fight. And those who want to leave? It's best to let them go. We could spend all our days chasing them down and trying to appease them when we could be strategically pursuing the vision. I want to chase after the people who are truly lost without salvation, not the ones who are saved who want to be churched elsewhere. That's hard for me as a person and as a minister. I am a natural sanguine and when someone doesn't like me, well, it hurts my feelings.

So be it. That's all part of taking on the attitude modeled to us by Jesus.

In the end, it was the salvation of our church. Certain things had to die so we could be set free to live. We were standing at a critical junction in the history of Brand New Church. It was hard to see them walk away, but when the dust settled months later, 100 percent of everyone who stayed was 100 percent on board. We were ready to move ahead without apology. Yes, it hurt, but it had to be done.

6
LEADERSHIP

Leadership:
Resisting the Urge to Settle

Not that I have already obtained all this, or have already been made perfect, but I press on to take hold of that for which Christ Jesus took hold of me. Brothers, I do not consider myself yet to have taken hold of it. But one thing I do: Forgetting what lies behind and straining toward what is ahead, I press on toward the goal to win the prize for which God has called me heavenward in Christ Jesus (Phil. 3:12–14).

An ancient Chinese proverb says, "He who thinks he leadeth and has no one following is only taking a walk." You're nodding your head, aren't you! Yeah, everybody gets it. The problem is that most of us are living it. In our homes, in our churches, and even in our own personal lives, the vast majority of us are experiencing a lack of leadership. And that's just tragic. God has so many gifts inside all of us that are ready to bloom. In Christ, we have been given an attitude of change and sacrifice, and yet it seems to be going nowhere. Why? Why do we settle for average, for the mundane, for the way it's always been done, for the "same old same old" attitudes? I believe it's because people are basically "satisfied." We have become comfortable and complacent, putting our God-given vision on the back burner. I say, "Enough of that!" It's time to lead again.

I have narrowed down "leadership" to this simple definition: LEADERSHIP IS . . . resisting the urge to SETTLE.

Leadership emerges when someone has had enough, when they say change must take place, and when they're willing to stand up and be used by God to make a difference.

Leadership is both taught and brought. It is taught in the sense that someone, at one time, showed a leader what leadership looks like by standing up to make a difference. Leadership is also "brought" in the sense that it doesn't just show up, you have to bring it! It doesn't happen by default; it happens by choice when someone catches a vision, seizes the opportunities, and then bends the knee before God as a willing servant to do His will. Some of the greatest leaders on our staff were taught leadership before they brought it. Only a few brought it first, but those who did were put on the forefront of our church. One of our biggest challenges, however, is that we live in a world that teaches us to expect a reward before we put in the effort:

What the World Teaches Us

- We want to have a great family life before learning to be great parents and spouses.

- We want to grow a congregation, rather than growing congregants.

- We want to be followed before we know how to lead.

That's not the way it works. Authentic leadership, whether it is in the home, the church, or within you, does not come automatically with time, title, or position. It must be won. And it must be won one person at a time, one by one by one — no shortcuts.

Leadership is an indispensable attribute of bringing true VALUE to the rural church. When someone resists the urge to settle and stands up to make a difference, the hope of God is unleashed into action. It doesn't matter if the difference appears to be huge or minuscule, or if it comes from the presidency, the pulpit, or the nursery. With growing leadership, based on godly, biblical principles, we can reach our communities, our country, and our world. But true leadership actually starts much closer than that. Leadership doesn't begin in some remote corner of the mission field, or at the heights of some political office. It starts, actually, in the home.

LEADERSHIP 101:
Resisting the Urge to Settle in the Home on the Range

It is so easy to hide in a big church in a metro area. You can hide in the back row, you can hide in the choir, and you can hide behind your secretary in your office. There is no immediate intimacy with your community. In a large church in a large community you can hide in the masses. You'll probably never meet the person in the apartment above or below you; you never get the name of the person who sits in the pew behind you. You're not shopping with them, not playing ball with their kids, not going to the same hospital or doctor as them.

Living in the rurals is totally different. It's like living in the proverbial fishbowl. Out here in the sticks, they will see me and my family and my marriage more than they ever will in the city. They are the same ones I see at the movies, at the band concert, at the barbershop. I'm becoming more and more convinced that leadership in the rural church has little to do with what happens on the stage and everything to do with what happens on the stage of life in the public arena, because in rural America, there really is very little that's private. Everybody knows your wife, everybody knows your kids, everybody knows your junk, and everybody knows your marriage.

That's why I'm convinced that leadership must begin in the home. My life, my wife, and my marriage have got to be red hot, because a red-hot marriage and a functional family is the most powerful evangelistic tool in rural America. I know that sounds like an exaggeration, but I really believe it. More important than the building, than the satellite uplinks, than the Christmas cantata is what's happening in the home, because everyone sees it and it speaks volumes about the gospel.

I did a series one time on parenting and family. I asked, "What is your vision for your family?" No one had one. Seriously. No one. Some seemed to have some vague ideas: we want "good" kids, we hope they graduate, and we hope they don't embarrass us in Wal-Mart. (And just for the record, your teen is hoping you won't embarrass him in Wal-Mart either! Finally something you can agree on!) That is about the extent of the vision most parents have for their families or their marriages. What a waste! Because God is totally into marriage, and totally into the family, this stuff is totally God-designed.

God spoke marriage into being. He said, "It is not good for the man to be alone" (Gen. 2:18). Yeah, Adam had it all in the Garden of Eden, the ultimate bachelor pad, but it wasn't right, so with bone of his bone and flesh of his flesh, God completed the picture perfectly.

God gave away the first bride. When God presented Eve to Adam, and when God presents us with our spouse, He does so passionately, intentionally, and out of the ultimate goodness of His sovereign will. Receiving the gift of our spouse is not an option; it's an imperative that sends shock waves throughout both the Old and New Testament in our lives today.

God established the one-flesh union. Yeah, sex is His idea, too. Leave the father and mother and become one flesh in such a powerful and passionate way that it becomes an earthly symbol of the heavenly love Christ has for the Church.

We should be adamant about echoing to those in our sphere of influence what God has designed to bring glory to Him. It's a mandate, not an invitation. It's a *call* — an inseparable aspect of the vision and attitude of Christ. Earthly marriage is a picture of heavenly marriage. We are the bride. He is the groom. Marriage is a declaration to a lost world about how effective salvation is. You must be dedicated to a red-hot marriage or your ministry will not survive.

But in reality, most of us have given in to the urge to settle. We've given up on the ideal. We are complacently enduring at best, and bailing out altogether at worst. Why? Well, because marriage is tough, and it can be very painful. Words stab us in the heart and in the back. The roller coaster of relationship struggles can make us feel nauseous as we ride out the same struggles over and over again. It can seem like a never-ending battle with nothing to gain and everything to lose.

If you found yourself at this point, I'm calling you, in the name of God, to resist the urge to settle! I know from years of personal experience that it's always easy to blame the problems on my wife, and it's equally easy for her to blame all of our problems on me. But in reality, if we're having problems, we are having problems with God, and not with each other. We're always hoping that *they* will change when the real issue is a God issue and a leadership issue.

Learn how to avoid "settling" by watching
"Audience of One" at **www.nlpg.com/bnc.**

Now is the time to believe God in being
true to the call He has given us, and allow
this truth to be our benchmark.

Man Up

I get asked a lot of questions at the marriage conferences we do. "How much can we, you know, should we be, you know, doing *it*." "What do you think about, umm, well, role play in the bedroom?" I have an opinion about that one, actually. I know this guy who dressed up in a Superman costume and was "flying" from the dresser to the bed to rescue his wife who was handcuffed to the headboard when he got knocked out cold by the ceiling fan. Out of reach of the phone, all his wife could do was yell for help from the neighbors, who called the fire department, who broke down the door and found them, well. Yeah, explain that one to your mother-in-law. But I digress (understatement). Let me start over.

I get asked a lot of questions at the marriage conferences we do. But there is one question that I'm asked more often than any other — and it's one that pierces my heart like nothing else. After the crowd has cleared out, a man walks up to me and says, "Shannon, I don't know how to be the spiritual leader of my home. How do you do that?" I both love and hate that question. I love it because it reveals an instinctive drive that simmers within every man to be a godly leader of his household. And I hate it because so few men feel they have permission to be that leader, and fewer still know how to do it. But praise God, because the men who are asking this question are resisting the urge to settle and they're willing to take some risks and make some changes to be who God has created them to be.

Now this book is primarily about growing the rural church, and I feel that having a red-hot marriage and a functional

family is an extremely important element of that, but there's
no way that I can cover in a couple of pages everything a man
needs to take up leadership in this area. But let me answer the
question with a few things, and then encourage you to go to
our website for a list of materials, conferences, and messages
that will help you jump-start the lifelong process of becoming
the leader that God wants to be through you.

First, the word "husband" means "houseman" and
"headship," and the Bible has a lot to say to the husband,
primarily:

> Husbands, love your wives, just as Christ loved the church
> and gave himself up for her (Eph. 5:25).

The man's position of leadership in the home positions
him to love as Christ loved the church. What did Jesus do
for the Church? He lived for it. He was judged for it. He was
condemned for it. He was bruised and bloodied to the point
where He could not be identified as a man for it. He walked up
the Via Dolorosa for it. And then, under the scorn and mocking
of a crowd in the blistering sun, He died for it.

That's the answer. Any more questions?

Really, everything else is a sub-point of that one answer. It's
the same answer we found in Colossians 3 where Paul exhorts
us to have the same attitude that was in Christ Jesus. That's the
type of leadership that we are being called to. The main focus of
our marriage is not to stay "in love." The main focus of marriage
is obedience to God because He has called you to continue
to love regardless. That's the bottom line. Please listen closely:
many of you think that your marriage is sufficient if you *feel* in
love. That's not what we are called to. Learn from Gethsemane.
Did Jesus *feel* like going to the Cross? No. He was in agony,
physically stressed to the point of sweating blood. If you're
getting close to sweating blood in your marriage, you're getting
close to what God experienced in the person of Jesus Christ. If
you're not, you still have a long way to go. Is that ridiculous?
Yeah, but only if you are listening to Oprah rather than God's

Word. I've heard and understand all of the "yeah, buts": Yeah, but she's just not meeting my needs. Yeah, but she doesn't respect me. Yeah, but . . . Yeah but . . .

Dear God, what if Jesus had made a list like that? He said that He loved the world so much that He was going to bleed and die for it. No condition. Just headship under obedience. That's the standard of leadership in the home, and that standard of leadership rests on the *houseband* (what the word "husband" means); it always has.

Go back to Genesis 3 for just a few minutes. You know the story. In early Eden, all was very, very good. However, the deceiver tempts Eve and she brings the forbidden apple to Adam that they both willingly eat. And then they are afraid — and so are most men today. Many of us are hearing the sound of the Lord right now, walking through the garden of our minds. So many of us are carrying the stains of disobedience, of not supporting His mission, of not leading our families, and we are hiding. We try to sweep it under the rug, we don't want to talk about the porn, or the affair, or why we don't pray. . . . After all, Eve started it, right? Maybe, but the Lord called to the man, *"Adam, where are you?"* The Lord God Almighty knew who ate first; He knew who committed the sin of adultery on the truth of God. He doesn't point to the woman. He points to the man, the one who holds the responsibility of headship. Today He looks at men and asks the same question: *Where are you? Where are you? Somebody must lead! For the hope of the gospel of Jesus Christ and the message of the glorification of the Church, somebody must lead a red-hot marriage.*

Is that fair? Absolutely not. God is not fair. God is just. God is not subjected to our commentary or ideology. He doesn't care about what we think about marriage. He knows what is true about His love for the Church and the loving leadership of the man in the family. Leadership is resisting the urge to settle, and leadership in the home is resisting the urge to settle for a lack of provision and protection in a family. Because of who Jesus is within us, He has equipped us in every good thing to do His will, that which is pleasing in His sight (Heb. 13:21). Now, let me be a little bit more specific about what He wants to accomplish through you:

What God Wants to Accomplish Through You

1. Spiritual provision

2. Physical provision

3. Spiritual protection

4. Physical protection

Spiritual provision. Reading the Scriptures, praying, confessing your sins and asking for forgiveness, extending forgiveness, and initiating service, ministry, and worship opportunities. The Holy Spirit inside of you is ready to work these things out of you.

Physical provision. "If anyone does not provide for his relatives, and especially for *his* immediate family, he has denied the faith and is worse than an unbeliever" (1 Tim. 5:8 emphasis added). God is the giver and provider of all things, and He can choose to do that through both you and your wife. But man, if you are not the primary breadwinner of the home, it will neuter you in the leadership of your home. Live within your means; give up the game of impressing your neighbors or indulging yourself. Whatever you do, do it heartily for the Lord, and not for men. Become the man by leading financially as the head of your home.

Spiritual protection. When you lead with the love of Jesus at home, it protects your wife in the street. I know that men are so shocked when women become emotionally attached to someone else. This most often happens when there is a vacuum of emotional affection and affirmation at home. Provide for her heart and you will help protect her spirit. The same goes for your daughters and your sons.

Physical protection. Men, even if your wife has a black belt in jujitsu, you still take the lead as the protector. Insecurity is not an option for God's kids. God provides a security of protection to us as an eternal hope. You need to provide for your wife the hope of being protected. That's more than locks and guns. That means you guard their hearts, too. Do you hear a prowler in the night? Just show up at the door with a baseball bat and boxers, and that will be enough to scare most people off (not the bat as much as the boxers).

Women, Too

Ladies, it's your turn. Leadership is the ultimate responsibility of the man, but it doesn't let you off the hook. If you want to enhance, facilitate, and encourage your husband to be the man that God (and probably you) truly want him to be, there are some things you can do that will really help, and there are some things that you can stop doing that are making a difficult task even harder for him.

We start with an obvious one: if you want your husband to embrace change, you're not going to help him by nagging, complaining, pushing, or dragging. You're just working against a man's instincts when you do this. If a man becomes a true leader with a wife who's breathing down his neck all the time, he will do so *in spite of* her and not *because of* her. Get off his back and it will be easier for him to stand tall and take ownership of what he needs to do. A quiet spirit and a strong soul will help him to move mountains. But he will dig in his heels and die on a molehill before he will ever be truly changed by manipulation and complaining.

Just as he is called to love you as Christ loves the church, you are called to submit to him as to the Lord. If you read the Book of Proverbs, it'll tell you that it's better to live on the roof than with the constant drip of a nagging woman. At the same time, it's critical to understand what submission is *not:*

What Submission Is Not

→ Agreeing with everything that your husband says. It means agreeing with every word that God says.

→ Leaving your brain at the altar on your wedding day. You're an active part of the union as the two become one. Differing roles? Defined responsibility and authorities? Absolutely. Brainless and subservient? Absolutely not.

→ Putting the will of the husband above of the will of Christ. As a daughter of the God of the universe, your job is always to obey God first.

→ The woman acting out of fear; it is acting out of Christ's strength.

And let me tell you one more: *submission is not an umbrella for abuse.* If a husband ever abuses his wife in the name of submission, send the jerk to jail.

Well then, what is submission? Submission is *sub*-mission. It's the mission beneath the mission. It's an intentional, underlying support of the vision of the leader. Those of you who are on staff as women? You need to make sure you are doing your part to support the mission of the church as well as the vision of your husband. I know you have your own set of "yeah, buts." Yeah, but he doesn't have a mission. Yeah, but my husband won't take the initiative. Yeah, but . . . yeah, but . . . Listen, give the guy some space and start by training like crazy for him. Your support might refresh his vision for his mission.

So how do you bring your man into leadership potential? *Without words.* God can do this. He doesn't need your help. In fact, it's possible that God might be waiting for you to back off and quit trying to play God in his life. You are not in control of that man. God is. If you live in conscious rebellion, contrary to God's Word on this point (or any other point!), you better ask yourself if you are truly repentant, redeemed, transformed, and saved. Rather than ask how you can manipulate your husband into being the kind of man you want him to be, it might be better to ask, "Has the metamorphosis taken place in my life that yields me to a Christ-centered life, disciplined to the holy Word of God, and powered by the Holy Spirit?" I'm telling you, if you want your husband to lead, release the guy and let God have His way. God doesn't need your help on this one. He probably just needs you to get out of the way so He can do His thing.

First Things First

When it comes to marriage, family, and ministry in the rural church, we've got to keep our priorities straight. This might sound strange in a book that hopes to get you pumped up about the potential of the churches in the boonies, but church growth is actually last on your list of most important priorities. God comes first, then marriage, then the kids, then your vocation, then your church.

Keeping everything balanced out is always a juggling act, the kind of organizing that husbands and wives can do together. Cindy and I do this week by week. Sunday night we open our calendars and BlackBerrys and make our plan of attack. Our goal is to have three meals together as a family each week. Doesn't always happen, but that's our goal. We schedule our date nights together, because those will never happen unless we plan on it happening. And then we start to fill in with church meetings, kids' programs, etc.

If you're looking for a natural place to bring prayer into your relationship, this is a good place to start. Bring God into the weekly planning process: thank Him for what He has already provided, ask for His direction, and submit together to His will for your family. Hey, you have to start somewhere. Men, if your marriage is strained and struggling, this is as good a place to start as any. Pastors' wives have said to me, "My husband hasn't prayed with me or led me spiritually our entire ministry. He has prayed with a lot of people and for a lot of marriages, but not ours."

I worked with another pastor for 17 years, whose marriage was a mess. When it got to the point where he and his wife felt like everything was over, they came to me for counseling, both carrying a heavy weight of division, desperation, and discouragement. I looked at the wife and asked, "How many times did your husband pray with you at home other than at mealtimes or special events? The answer came back, "Zero." They started praying together and it brought about an immediate transformation. Yeah, there was still plenty to work out, but when he took the lead to bring his wife and family into prayer, they followed, and everything began to change, because with God in the picture, anything can happen. He is the one who knows how to take something that looks and stinks like a pile of manure and turn it into something beautiful and flourishing.

A Lesson From the Manure Pile

When I was a young child, we had a chore at our home called "the compost pile." The concept was pretty simple: collect all the organic junk you can find — food scraps, leaves, animal dung — all the stuff that can decay, and then pile it up. My friend Bruce Medley has the ultimate compost pile on the planet. He heaps up semi-truckloads of manure and dead chickens on his property. Yes, he does this on purpose. In time it becomes this massive smoldering mess. On a warm, humid day that thing smells like the bowels of hell have smelted themselves on his land — even worse than the basement bathrooms in our old church . . . but not as bad as some marriages.

Listen, I'm not going to present the ideal of a red-hot marriage without acknowledging that a normal marriage can accumulate a lot of stinking, rotting junk from the past. Broken expectations, unfulfilled desires, shattered promises, cutting words, acts of betrayal . . . a marriage is the perfect place to build a compost pile of pain, frustration, and anger. Relive the offenses, hold on to the hurt, dwell on the injustices, and pretty soon you have a massive, smoldering, stinking mass.

But there's a miracle in the manure pile and there are miracles waiting to happen in marriages. Compost piles, when handled properly, produce some of the richest, most fertile soils and fertilizers on the planet. Take something that was dead and watch God give it life, using it to grow something new, green, and luscious. Take the pain of your dead marriage and bring it to God, and watch Him heal, liberate, and breathe into it something brand new.

> When you were dead in your sins and in the uncircumcision of your sinful nature, God made you alive with Christ. He forgave us all our sins, having canceled the written code, with its regulations, that was against us and that stood opposed to us; he took it away, nailing it to the cross (Col. 2:13–14).

Christ has done that for you, and if your spouse is a believer, He has done it for him or her as well. But in order to turn a manure pile of a marriage into the fertilizer for a red-hot marriage, you must allow that same forgiveness of Christ to flow from you to your spouse as well. Take the pain, take the offenses, dig them up with a spade, and spread them at the feet of the Cross, releasing them and leaving them there with your Lord. Let go, because He knows what to do. He is in the business of taking things that are dead and giving them new life.

Transparency

Life and leadership in the home and growing rural churches
are inseparable. Having a red-hot marriage and a functional
family is more important in rural America than anywhere
else if you want your life to be a message of the gospel. A
growing ministry? Yes, but the marriage comes first . . . and you
don't have a good marriage for the sake of a growing church.
Marriage is not just a means to that end. It's not a side effect,
it's the prize. It's the reward for being able to live in a small
community where secrets are few and lives are so transparent.
What a privilege it is to be honest and real and let people see
that, though far from perfect, Christ is having His way in your
home, and it is good. Don't settle for an average marriage or for
status quo in the church.

Leadership 201:
Resisting the Urge to Settle with the Church

He showed up late again, as usual, and slid into the back
row of our North campus, unshaven and smelling of cigarettes
with just a hint of stale beer. It was a really demanding season
in the journey of our church, for me at least. Everyone else was
really enjoying the ride, but at that point I felt like I was doing
everything. *A lot easier to pastor a fully staffed metro church,* I
thought. *It's hard to cast vision when you're cleaning the coffee cups
and trying to balance the checkbook. . . .* The guy in the back row
looked like a real piece of work, and he looked like a lot of extra
work for me — a major "project" that I just didn't have time for.

But the guy just kept showing up; I really had no idea why.
He was so out of place in so many different ways He was three
decades younger than our average 60-year-old attendee; he wore
work clothes rather than the established code of "Sunday best";
and he obviously had no clue how to talk and act in order to fit
into the Christian subculture. *Doesn't he have anything better to*

do on a Sunday morning? Shouldn't he be sleeping something off or something? Apparently he didn't.

If I had known then what I know now about the guy in the back row, I would have dropped everything, *everything,* on my agenda and pulled that guy into my life and into our church from day one. But I didn't, because when I was in seminary they never taught me about the guys in the back row. I knew that we needed help, but the kind of help I was looking for didn't come in packages like this — at least that's what I had been taught. Still, he kept coming. I started to get to know him, and finally, even though I didn't think I had the time for it, I invited him into our home. . . .

I've learned a lot since then, and he has become an important leader in our worship experience. Change can come in many different ways and packages. And the best ones come from people within your own congregation.

The Problem

Rural America is in the middle of a massive drought — a spiritual drought caused by a lack of vision, attitude, and leadership. The fields might be flourishing and green, but when it comes to the state of the Church, it is a dusty, dry land. Do rural churches have the leadership quotient to take them to the next level? The answer is usually no. In fact, that's been the answer for so long that few people even ask the question anymore. If salary, buildings, budgets, and perks aren't available to draw great leadership into your community, what do you do then? Give in to the urge to settle? Yeah, that's what you do. Just give up. You can't do anything about it anyway. Lack of leadership has always been a problem in rural churches. We are always getting the leftovers anyway, the hand-me-down pastors that nobody else wants anymore. So we might as well get used to hand-me-down churches.

Are you standing on a precipice of indecision? View "Plant Your Feet" at **www.nlpg.com/bnc.**

Is it time to walk away or time to plant your feet and stand strong against forces that want to sideline the mission of your ministry?

It's time to break that rule about the rurals. No, let's do better than that: let's *shatter* it. Brand New Church had no paid positions for three and a half years. Cindy and I were paid enough to get by, but other than that, we didn't have any paid staff until I hired an eight-dollar-an-hour secretary part-time to answer the phone. During that time, God caused amazing growth by providing amazing leadership for our body. But one more time, He worked in obscurity; He defied conventional wisdom and did something new.

When I was interviewing at a church in Oklahoma, the leadership gave three requirements for any potential candidate: (1) seminary education, (2) five years of ministry experience, and (3) must be married. I didn't even question it at the time because that's the way everybody always does it. It later dawned on me that Jesus couldn't get a job at that church! He would have flunked every single requirement.

When we give in to thinking like that, we give in to the urge to settle. Let's break that rule by looking at the Principles, the Plan, and the Power of developing thriving leadership in the rural church . . . or any church for that matter.

The Principles of Leadership

1. **A leader is anyone who resists the urge to settle.** That means leadership comes in packages of potential that take on many different shapes and sizes. *Anyone* who resists complacency has the potential for leadership.

2. **Leadership is born out of life change.** Leaders emerge when someone's life is transformed on the inside, not when you bring in a hired gun from the outside. Therefore, leadership is not professional, it's personal.

3. **Your best leaders are sitting in your pews.** Listen carefully to that one, because I'm not saying that you can "get by" with the leaders in your congregation; I'm saying that they are your *best* leaders. Just because you can't pay for somebody doesn't mean you're getting second best.

I have hired staff from the outside, but they have not worked for us here. When you are working rural, you can't just bring somebody in who has worked in a big church and expect him to adapt to a rural community. Also, most church staff members do not want to work hard. Ministry breeds laziness and too much specificity. At Brand New Church you have to be able to do it all. If you play the guitar, great, but we need you to clean toilets today and mow tomorrow. If you can teach, great; we need you to help wax the floors and set up the youth room next week.

It all goes back to vision.

Clearly articulated and passionately proclaimed vision causes leadership to rise up within the ranks and calls more soldiers to the cause. You can't buy that. The people you attract with money are little more than ministry mercenaries. What you need are people who will give their lives for the vision no matter what it costs.

Listen, if you aren't casting vision, the only ones who will want to serve with you are those who are interested in maintaining control of the status quo. Besides that, everybody in the congregation will assume that you can handle it on your own, and that you should handle everything on your own, because you're the one getting paid to do it. They'll just become consumers and participants and never step up to lead. That is why another Sunday school class or another Bible study is sometimes (but not always) a detriment because we are just feeding them again instead of equipping them to serve.

If you don't have vision, you will not attract leaders at any price. Let there be no doubt that the vision of the leader becomes the vision of the church. **A church that has vision will see leadership emerge from within as long as:**

∽   the pastor is willing to delegate;

∽   teams are structured around a mission; and

∽   staff is designated according to clear biblical principles.

All of this has its roots in the commitment by the church's leadership to grow congregants rather than a congregation. This is one of the most important principles in rural church mission. We build people, not organizations. If we build organizations, we will end up with buildings and programs that serve only themselves. As you start growing congregants, all of a sudden all these things you never thought you would have start to appear. Congregant after congregant begins to fill the leadership void — that is, if you have a plan.

The Plan
Delegation to All

In Exodus 18, we find Moses getting an earful from his father-in-law, Jethro. Jethro was excited to hear about everything that God was doing, but he could clearly see that Moses was being worn down by all the responsibilities. His advice? "Select capable men from all the people — men who fear God, trustworthy men who hate dishonest gain — and appoint them as officials over thousands, hundreds, fifties and tens" (Exod. 18:21).

If I were standing there that day, which assignment would I receive? What qualified someone to lead thousands? What qualified someone to lead tens? It's not entirely clear from the text, but the model of sharing workload with capable people is timeless and indispensable if you're going to grow a rural church. And people are all waiting in the pews or chairs or benches to grab hold of the vision and the work. If you have vision, you will have too many people wanting to do stuff. The rural pastor has to know the people he needs are not at the First Big Baptist down the road or Monster Methodist across the county. They are sitting in the pews (or in our case, the chairs). And they are waiting. Just cast the vision. Have them in your home. Eat with them. Build relationships, relationships, relationships. You are going to find out what their giftedness is and draw it out from within. That's the best way, and that's the only way. Unless you are sitting on an oil well, you have no choice, but I'm telling you, given the choice, I would rather raise up a leader from within my body than try to buy one from the outside any day.

From time to time, however, I have brought in a person or two from outside our church. I get them for a minimal number of dollars and they stay for a minimal amount of time to train and educate our body. They raised the bar, so to speak, so that the congregation could see what it looks like done right. It would stir up within the congregation some desire and some talent, and they would follow the example and begin to do great stuff, such as children's worship — which, by the way, is the first position you want to pray to fill. If you are going to staff a rural church, the first position is not worship and it's not a youth pastor. The first position is children. When our children's ministry took on the first staff person, it was not only without pay, but that individual started investing personal money in the program. When people catch a vision, they do some crazy stuff.

Some pastors will struggle with this, having a hard time giving up the control and the kudos that come with doing everything. But if you're humble enough to share the work, and tired enough to give up the load, your congregation will respond to the vision. I used to have to go to the hospital all the time. Now Shain gets there before I find out someone is even

Volunteers are a vital part of BNC

sick. That gave me more time to spend with people like Bill, who came to Christ and brought his wife, Jane, along with him. She is a stay-at-home mom but her kids go to school from eight to three. She was a clerical assistant for five years and now she comes in and answers the phone for us. Huge burden removed and a vital job now getting done with excellence.

By communicating the vision, expressing the needs, and opening the door to capable volunteers, things started to take off like crazy. The next thing we knew we had 60 or 70 kids showing up on Wednesday nights (from a town of 88, I remind you). At first, I watched everything like a hawk and worked hard to help my volunteers develop their leadership skills. The first thing I said to them was, "Find someone just like you to take your place!" They did, and this allowed us to either multiply our efforts or to move on to new areas of opportunity. It was just way cool. (It still is!)

Volunteers are the heartbeat of Brand New Church. Whatever happens well during a weekend experience begins with volunteers in the parking lot, then greeters, cafe, retail services, children, preschool, ushers, hosts, campus support, first impressions, bomb squad (stage hands), worship team, tech team (switchers, media, editing, cameras, lighting, audio, and more), iCampus, student ministry, emerge, bus ministry. . . . Our volunteers don't just fill a ministry position for the church; our volunteers live the mission of the church. It makes me cry just thinking about it.

What makes a great VOLUNTEER?

Vision. If an organization does not have continuing vision, it will never have the excellence needed in any area. Church members do not respond to need, they respond and sign up for vision.

Opportunity. Every human wants to make a difference. We must make volunteering easily available to everyone attending our churches. Options for volunteering should be available to everyone, both maturing and mature believers, and even those who haven't come to know the Lord yet.

Leadership. Each area should have an excellent leader with passion and faithfulness. This is the key to success for any area of volunteering. We do not have "paid" leaders, but the most unbelievable volunteer leaders are overseeing each area of leadership. Our campus pastors are then responsible to educate and keep the vision awareness in front of the teams.

Unanswered. Clarity and communication are key. No question will go unanswered. When our volunteers need to know something, their leaders must have an answer. If someone asks our volunteers a question, they need to know the answer or how to find someone who does.

Transit. Constantly, consistently, and continually transmit the vision, mission, and our preoccupation with reaching the lost. This must be seen in every area and in every attention to detail.

Environment. In every gathering that we have, we believe that something eternal is taking place. It's so important that we must make every effort to create an excellent environment. This happens three ways: (1) sight — we must have excellent aesthetics and a clutter-free facility; (2) sound — this can remove awkwardness for first timers, promote relaxation in children's areas, and provide a listening ear during the worship through song experience; (3) smell — smell is often the first impression, so make certain your campus has a concentrated focus and soothing, unobtrusive scents.

Relationships. Your volunteer teams will become a family by meeting each other's needs — hospital visits, baby showers, encouragement, and so much more. We are finding that our volunteer teams are becoming the premiere connecting point of our church family.

In rural America, delegation is a must! The leaders in the volunteers are waiting, but knowing when and what to delegate is a sensitive and Spirit-filled decision. Here are some suggestions for getting started:

1. Make a list of what you need and want to do for the next two weeks. So many of us struggle because we simply don't know what we need to do day in and day out.

2. Identify "priority tasks" that can be delegated. Please note that there is a big difference between busy work and worthy work. A great leader or volunteer will not stay with you when busy work is assigned regularly.

3. Pray and pray more about who! You need a loyal leader who can handle the pressure. Do not approach them with a job to take stuff off your plate. Share the opportunity to make a difference. People everywhere want to make a difference!

4. Pray more and publicize less. Some of the most willing are not always the most qualified. Some of your best will need to be approached by you, rather than solicited by everyone.

5. Be specific. Have the assignment clear, concise, and calendared. Make certain they are clear about deadlines (I struggle with this).

6. Empower the person. Give him or her the authority to do the job! Let him or her in on decisions and direction of the task. They need ownership.

7. Give them an OUT! Determine a review date so they

can get out or you can graciously let them out. This is
IMPORTANT!

8. Maintain accountability and communication. If they are
not accountable and contacted regularly they will fade. Love
them enough to encourage and support them in the task.

9. Gratitude! Be grateful — use thank-you notes, calls, and
public celebration.

10. Take Note: You might be training a future staff member.
You are certainly shaping character in his or her life.

Back in the day, a handful of volunteers kept Brand New
Church moving and kept me sane. Now the hundreds of
volunteers that are pouring their lives into the mission are
truly the core of everything that God is doing. There is simply
no way, this could not have happened through paid positions.
Our volunteers do it better, they do it faster, and they do it
from the heart. Thank you, BNC volunteers, for setting the
bar for churches around the country in excellence, service, and
faithfulness to Jesus' mission to build His Church. You are the
best that money can't buy.

Designing Teams. Many churches, their leaders, and their
pastors are "stuck" with a polity structure that is committee
driven. Though I disagree with this approach in most (but
not all) organizations, it is still possible to develop visionary
leadership appropriately and biblically. It's really up to the
leader to determine how a committee is going to operate. I
strongly encourage you to develop and design teamness within a
committee. Committees that have been changed into teams are
powerful. What is the difference between a committee and
a team?

Committees	Teams
debate issues	deliver results
discuss problems	drive solutions
give in to the urge to settle	lead by their vision and attitude

In six years as pastor I have found that "ministry positions" and committees breed laziness. That is why we stopped focusing on "ministry" and are all about the MISSION. (On the other hand, if you have a program that you want to kill, delegate it to a committee, or better yet a subcommittee of that committee! You will probably never hear from them again. Though it's probably more humane to pull the plug on a program like that, rather than watch it die a slow, painful death . . .) If you want to make the shift from a committee mentality to mission team movement, here are a few suggestions:

Eight Ways of Becoming a Team

1. **Be very strategic when determining who serves on each team.** Use individuals who are already serving in your organization. They will be the ones who can make a difference.

2. **Share all the details.** Great leaders will serve as a team if they have clear instructions and know what they are doing. If they do not know the purpose or the passion behind the objective, it will be a committee, not a team.

3. **Be the tone setter.** You need to be very involved in creating the tone, environment, and outlook before the committee becomes a team. You have heard it said, and it is *very* true, "People respond to vision, not need." If your tone suggests vision, direction, influence, and making a difference, they will move past agenda-setting to action steps.

4. **Get with your team leaders often.** Your team will go back to a committee if it is disconnected from the leader. Monthly meetings, at the least, and a yearly retreat will grow the relationship and the effectiveness of a committee to a team.

5. **Meet in a place with some atmosphere.** Get out of the office, the boardroom, the dingy Sunday school classroom (with the map of Israel and the Royal Ambassadors pledge on the wall) and meet in your home or a relaxing place of

business. Create a welcoming relational environment that encourages creativity and freshness. Showing them that you are thinking through every detail of the meeting place will tell them you have prayed through every detail being presented (which you have, right?!).

6. **Create a Mission Group.** This is a team of leaders that gathers to dream and scheme about the future of the church. This will remove the control factor and create the Christ-like factor in your church or organization.

7. **Keep tenure short.** Do not let people serve on the same committee/team for long periods of time. Control and cruise control will take place nine times out of ten if a person (especially the wrong person) is left on a committee too long.

8. **Meet when there is no meeting.** Have leaders in your home, call them on the phone, and get them involved in your social network online when there is no meeting to announce. Love is the key to bridging a committee to a team!

In this type of team environment, you'll find that more and more committed people begin to emerge from the pews. These are your "deacons," the servant-leaders who are the lifeblood of the body. Sometimes they will take the initiative in asking for a place to serve. Don't give them something that is too much up front too quickly. Just give them something small and then watch to discover their natural leadership quotient. By developing a delegation plan, you always have a post of service waiting for an eager beaver, whether it is greeting, parking lot, babies, or café. Do not place the wrong person in a position in haste. You can usually fill high-profile positions fast, but when you have the wrong person in the wrong place, it takes forever to get rid of him or her and it can be very painful. When someone comes up and says, "I want to teach!" Tell them, "Great! Here's the toilet cleaner. Come back in three months and I'll give you a broom." You find out fast who just wants to be up front and who really has the heart of the servant-leader.

Designating Overseers

As we have grown, it has been awesome to have the opportunity and the ability to designate certain servant-leaders to our staff and pastor team. As you'll see in a moment, our standards for this level of service reflect biblical standards, as well as proven character and experience that show they have the heart of the "episcopos," the bishop/pastor who can shepherd and protect the flock.

A gentleman approached me several years ago to tell me that he thought he had been called to be on our staff. Major red flag! First of all, anyone called to be on our staff would never have to tell us that. They would be demonstrating it through tireless and faithful service at the church. This has happened several times, but you know what? Everyone that has come to tell me they are called to be on staff ends up leaving instead. Time proved that they really didn't want to be on our staff, they just really wanted a great job (which our staff positions are!). In order to eliminate those looking for a job and find those who have a passion to serve at any cost, we've adopted a simple philosophy: nobody gets paid until we've seen that they are willing to do it for nothing . . . or less.

Fred Smith's story about the origins of FedEx reveals what we are talking about. Fred presented his model for worldwide overnight delivery service in his MBA thesis. He got an F, but he moved ahead on faith anyway, throwing everything he had into the idea. The vision caught on and his team took ownership. But it was rough going. Underfunded and overworked, it looked like the whole thing was going belly up. But the team wouldn't give up. His pilots believed in his vision so much they started taking out second mortgages and selling their cars to help make up for the million dollars they needed to keep running. A truck driver pulled his watch off and sold it to a pawnshop to get enough money to put fuel in his truck to get it back from Memphis.

That's the kind of mind set we need on our staff teams — we need those who will do whatever it takes to continue to grow even in the painful moments. It's an amazing thing to be a part of. During the heart-wrenching times, I lay beside my wife at night bawling my eyes out because of what people were willing to do, and do without, to fulfill the vision God laid before us.

If someone really wants to be on your staff, they may need to be willing to work at Burger King part-time to make it happen. It's not about pay. The whole paid pastor vocational deal is a wonderful thing, and Scripture teaches that you shouldn't muzzle the ox while he is treading the grain. We know that. But an ox that really wants to work will find a way, even if we can't pay a salary. Take David Jackson. He was a part of BNC for almost two years while on staff at another church. He would attend our 1:00 service after leaving the church he served. He played the keyboard for us sometimes. I knew that he played the guitar as well, and after about six months I said, "Why don't you help out and lead?" He did, and he not only proved his ability but his willingness to serve sacrificially. We observed this passion for about two years before we hired him on as the pastor of our Mountain Home campus.

As long as we're at it, let's break one more rule. This rule says pastors and staff need to have a seminary education, or at least have gone to Bible school. I believed that because that's what they told me at, well, seminary and Bible school, of course. It really makes me mad just to think about it. No one in the New Testament Church was educated. Acts 4:13 says they were "unschooled, ordinary men." The word "ordinary" is translated from *idiotace,* from which we get the English word "idiot." That is what it means. But the people saw that these early leaders had been with Jesus and had the vision and passion that He had entrusted to them.

Please don't misunderstand. Bible school or seminary education is the best thing you can do *if you are called to it.* I don't believe seminary is for every pastor. Some of it was very beneficial for me, but that's not what qualifies me to be a pastor. I can tell you the greatest seminary ever is when you wake up at 6:00 in the morning and you get on your knees and face before God and then you walk out and love on people. God's requirements are so different from the rules that permeate the Church today. What does someone need to be qualified as a pastor or staff person?

> Here is a trustworthy saying: If anyone sets his heart on being an overseer, he desires a noble task. Now the overseer must be above reproach, the husband of but one wife, temperate, self-controlled, respectable, hospitable, able to teach, not given to drunkenness, not violent but gentle, not quarrelsome, not a lover of money. He must manage his own family well and see that his children obey him with proper respect. (If anyone does not know how to manage his own family, how can he take care of God's church?) (1 Tim. 3:1–5).

Believe it or not, I was never taught this in seminary. Just in case you've never heard it either, I want to dissect a few of these MUST-HAVES for ministry:

1. **One Wife.** There is no greater picture of your walk, commitment, discipline, and passion for Jesus than in your marriage. Marriage is a picture of your salvation. If your marriage is red hot, your walk with God is red hot. The opposite is also true . . . cold equals colder.

2. **Hospitable.** I rarely spent time in my pastors' homes. We have, as pastors, the mentality that having guests in our home removes our effectiveness. I don't know the balance, but the Scripture is saying we must be "fond of guests." Cindy and I love having others in our home for intimate moments of fellowship. Hospitable is the word *hospital.* Are you a hospital for your church members? In a rural environment, this is a must!

3. **Able to Teach.** Every leader must be able to present God's truth. Don't misunderstand this as preaching, but apt to teach. Bishops must be able to open the Holy Word of God and "shuck the corn" with skill and with aptitude. Leaders must lead with their ability to "sell" God's vision for the mission. Teaching is connection, not just communicating. Your greatest moments of teaching might be at a dining table, on a fishing boat, or in a staff meeting. Your life, marriage, and family must teach without words.

4. **Not Quarrelsome.** More is done from within the Body of Christ to harm the message of Christ than outside the walls. Unfortunately, there are church leaders that kill the gospel and its power in a community by throwing other church leaders under the bus. Pastors may be top on the guilt list of this sin. That is why we must stay away from it.

5. **Children Obey Him.** The level of leadership found in a man is shown in his children. I am not saying perfection, but respect. The pastor's or deacon's kids jokes are an abomination to Christ's church. I know there are specific cases of uniqueness, but overall the parent must have leadership of the home to have leadership in his ministry.

In light of the clear teaching in this passage as well the experience we've gained along the journey, now we have restructured our staff requirements:

If married . . . a red-hot marriage. If single . . . how do they manage their personal self-disciplines (money, mouth, meals, motivation)? Are they "majorly" in debt, do they talk too much, are they "majorly" overweight (everyone who is big is not overweight), and are they a self-starter?

Relationship builder. If you don't love people, you are not called.

Passion for our God. This is found out from the people closest to them. (Numbers 2 and 3 are the staples of the Great Commission: love God and love people.)

Loyalty. Listen to how they talk about their previous employment and employer, their parents, their spouse, and their kids.

Understand God's Vision for Brand New Church. The word *understand* means submitting to what was stated. The potential staff must get "under" the pastor's vision and mission with no "agenda" of their own. They need ministry ideology and the skills to create new ministry, but they do so by "standing under" the direction of the senior pastor.

The Power

By understanding the problem, living by a handful of key principles, and executing a strategic plan, God can use you to unleash the incredible power of leadership that is waiting in the pews of your church and on the streets of your community. You probably have someone under your nose like Bruce Medley, the chicken farmer with a monster compost pile. *Chicken farmer? Compost pile?* Our culture automatically gives him two thumbs down, but I have built a relationship with this guy as I've hung out with him. We would go out to eat with him, and he would eat his sardines and crackers (which I would decline) and I would listen to his story. As I did I began to discover something about this man of the land: Bruce is a genius. He is probably an engineer without even knowing it. I started asking him, "Bruce, do you think you could____?" He would come up with an idea, we would attempt it, and then we would get it done. His persistence in inviting me to come to South Lead Hill has never waned. He has incredible faith and bulldog determination. Like most people, he has an official title, but on our staff team he does absolutely everything.

Cutting-edge technology is part of our branding at BNC, and we get our direction and influence from Zach Gilliam. I met Zach when he was a sixth grader in my student ministry back in Oklahoma. Even as a little kid, he displayed a willingness and ability to do cutting-edge stuff that I had no idea about. When I wanted to start using PowerPoint, he made it happen as a seventh grader. As an eighth grader and a freshman, he pulled off some crazy stuff for our youth group — I'm talking about multiple cameras at times, multiple video projectors at times. When we started to get a vision for iCampus and satellite churches, I immediately thought of Zach. He was in charge of all of the technology at BNC for several years. Lights, sound, Internet feeds, satellite uplinks . . . if he couldn't do it himself, he found someone who could make it happen. I guess that's what you would expect, though — after all, he did turn 21 this year, finally old enough to buy himself a beer if he wants.

Tony Knight was in my youth group years ago. I saw potential in him. He called me one day asking for prayer for his family and his future. He was leading worship part-time in a different state and I asked him to consider dumping it all and taking a risk to come work with us. He is now our pastor at our largest growing campus.

Every staff member I have has come from within BNC or from within my personal ministry. We've never advertised; we've never had a search committee. We are committed to growing congregants and not a congregation, applying the principles and a plan for leadership development. There is no need — and no desire — to go outside to find leaders. They were sitting in the pews all along, the most motivated, creative, devoted army of "idiots" that anyone could ask for.

Zach in the Back

Yeah, the drought of leadership in the churches of rural America has taught me a lot. Looking back at the journey so far, and looking ahead to where God might be taking us, I am so thankful that I was forced to break the rules. Back then, I didn't know that a leader is anyone who resists the urge to settle, that leadership is born out of life-change, and that the best leaders are already sitting in your pews — because that was before I

got to know that guy who was
sneaking into church late and
sliding into the back row.

He was another Zach,
a landscaper, addicted to
the same stuff a lot of other
people are. Just another blue-
collar guy working the dusty
roads of Arkansas trying to
make ends meet. When I
asked him to come over to
our home, he was so shocked
and so afraid that he almost bailed out.

Shannon & Zach Lee,
BNC's Worship Leader

Was I going to chew on him for leaving his cigarette butts in
the parking lot? Was this about the beer cans in the back of his
truck? No, I tried to assure him, I just wanted to share a meal
with him and hang out for a bit. We got to know each other
and even started to like each other. I found out that he had a
gift: he played the guitar — bluegrass. Not my favorite by any
means, but I thought, *What the heck, it can't hurt. Maybe he
will wake up the guy in the sound booth.* Shaking in his boots,
he stood up in front of all the gray hairs with his guitar and
played a couple songs, and then he played a couple more, and
then he began to lead worship. One of my fondest memories
in this whole journey is when I used to follow him down the
road on Sundays as we made the mad dash from the north
campus to the south campus. That old truck of his bouncing
over the potholes, smoke pouring out his windows, cigarette
butts bouncing off my windshield . . . Now he is in charge of
Creative Arts at all of our campuses and is, I believe, one of the
most passionate and gifted worship leaders in the country. He is
my brother — and it all started in the back row of a church that
smelled like mothballs.

Leadership 301:
Resisting the Urge to Settle in Our Personal Lives

A pastor friend called the other day. It was one of those calls that starts off with an enthusiastic, "Man, is it ever good to hear from you!" and ends in the shared agony of broken hearts, broken dreams, and broken lives. I never would have dreamed this in my wildest dreams, not from this friend at least, but he had $8,800 of Internet porn on his credit card.

He was so successful on the outside, yet so empty and so isolated on the inside — a tragic lesson in leadership, actually. Because, yes, leadership means resisting the urge to settle in our homes, and leadership means resisting the urge to settle in our churches. But perhaps more than all that, *leadership means resisting the urge to settle in our own personal lives.*

Let's be honest, leaders are natural targets for pride. As recognized "authorities" and "professionals," it's so easy to climb the ivory towers of our own imagination and look out at our work and our kingdoms as if they were our own creations. *Dear God, knock us off our pedestals and remind us that we are like everyone else: nothing but masses of flesh and arrogance were it not for Your grace, and Your mercy, and Your Spirit within us.*

Get Real

Let's face it, the vast majority of man-made Christian religion can survive just fine on a superficial level. Put on a Sunday smile, throw in a couple of Christian clichés, and we can navigate through our churches just fine. But God's not into the superficial; He's into what's real. He doesn't love what we do, He loves us, the real us. Part of the responsibility of leadership is being real about who we are in the Body (both the positive and the negative) and who we are as God's kids before the Father.

The Bible says that we are God's workmanship, created in Christ Jesus for good works that He prepared beforehand so that we can walk in them. Leadership can be transforming when we recognize how we were created and identify the specific works He has prepared us for. My niche is relationships. I love hanging out with people. I had seminary professors who would say, "Well, you need to drink coffee with the guys; you need to find out the price of cattle . . ." He thought he was being cliché, but just ask me now: I know the price of cattle! Thankfully, this positive aspect of my gifting served me well in the early days and still does. Perhaps the most important thing in the job description of a growing pastor is pouring life into the individuals of the church and community. Thankfully, that's what I'm good at; it comes absolutely naturally for me. One time I was trying to get to know one of our ranchers, but the guy was busy vaccinating his herd. The next thing I know I'm out there in the corral with one of those massive syringe guns in my hand, sticking cows in the butt. A lasting friendship was born through the sweat and the dirt and a job that needed to be done.

From music to lights, many talented people share their gifts at BNC.

Do you know your strengths? Do you know your gifting? If your gift is mercy, be at every hospital door every week. Do what you are good at. Start at room 101 and go to the end. Do what you do well. Pray over patients, over their families, over their kids. Next thing you know they are thinking, "Hey, we should check out that church." Why? Because you went to the hospital. Because you cared. Because you reached out to them with your spiritual gifts.

Bruce, on our staff, is one of the best funeral guys there is. He'd fail preaching lab but when he stands behind a casket or an urn, he reaches every person sitting in the audience. He just does a great job — a much better job than I do in that situation. Another staffer is a great counselor. I am a terrible counselor. He can love on someone and have their head spinning thinking they are the best person on earth before they turn around. I can't do that. Don't come to me for counseling unless you are super desperate. It's not one of my best gifts, *and I know that. Sure,* I try to improve in areas where I simply stink, *but I don't build a ministry around my weaknesses. I play to my strengths.*

Cliff Methvin and Bruce Medley, both original members of Southside and now elders at BNC.

And that brings us, again, to the most difficult questions that a pastor must ask of himself: *Am I gifted at this? Am I called to this?* It's important to ask those questions and to be able to answer with honesty. It's hard to say this, but I need to: I believe that often the average pastor in rural America is not called to pastor. That's probably hard to hear, but I've just seen it too many times. Many rural pastors take that job because Podunkville was the only opening they could find at the time, and they see it as some sort of a pit stop on the way toward larger and more visible ministry opportunities. I also think a lot of rural pastors were once great Sunday school teachers. So somebody in a leadership organization or denomination said, "Hey, there is a really sharp guy who loves the Lord teaching over here. Let's see if he could do this." So all of a sudden a good teacher gets thrown into the role of pastoring where he is forced to live outside of his gifting. Sadly, his true passion and calling as a teacher is forgotten.

Listen, a pastor has got to be sure that he is called to pastor. I'm not talking about preaching. There is a difference. A pastor is called to lead. It helps if you are also a good communicator, but you must be called and gifted to lead. A pastor is called to effectively cast vision. A pastor is called to shepherd. It is up to us as leaders to attract leaders. If you are struggling with attracting leaders, you must ask yourself if you *are* a leader. If you aren't a leader, then find one. You might have to give him the reins — even give him your title if necessary. Because a shepherd leads. He resists the urge to settle with his marriage and family, his church, *and* his personal life.

First Love First

There's no doubt about it, in order to have VALUE in ministry, we must have leadership. But along the road to a growing rural church, along that pathway to leadership, it is so easy for something to be tragically left behind in the dust of our ministry. The words of Jesus to the church of Ephesus in the

Book of Revelation are a sober warning to every church on the planet:

> I know your deeds, your hard work and your perseverance. I know that you cannot tolerate wicked men, that you have tested those who claim to be apostles but are not, and have found them false. You have persevered and have endured hardships for my name, and have not grown weary. Yet I hold this against you: You have forsaken your first love. Remember the height from which you have fallen! Repent and do the things you did at first. If you do not repent, I will come to you and remove your lampstand from its place (Rev. 2:2–5).

A leader cannot authentically lead someone if he is not legitimately headed in that direction himself. This is where the Christian faith differs from other professions, because we're not selling a product, we are engaged with a person, the person of Jesus Christ. He is the end and the means. We don't "do Jesus" to "get church." We just never graduate from the gospel. By God's grace and mercy, we grow and mature, but we never, ever cease to be little children in the arms of Abba, our Father. Our passions may develop, our vision may transform us, but our ministry — our lampstand — will be taken from us should we forsake Jesus, our first love.

 *The compass that controls your ministry will dictate its success. Take a moment and watch "Actively Growing" at* **www.nlpg.com/bnc** *as I stress the importance of a Christ-centered focus rather than traditions that sometimes just muddy the water.*

My dearest brothers and sisters, as you develop leadership and resist the urge to settle in your homes and in your churches, please, please resist the urge to settle in your personal relationship with Jesus Christ! Growing a church in rural America is an incredible journey, but it only makes sense when it is a byproduct of a personal, intimate, grace-based walk with the Son of God. Genuine leadership in a rural setting could be more important than it is in a metro setting, because out here you just can't fake it — at least not for very long!

For you have one Teacher, the Christ (Matt. 23:10).

7
UNDERSTANDING

Understanding:
Standing Under a Rock-Solid Structure

All authority in heaven and on earth has been given to me. Therefore go . . . (Matt. 28:18–19).

It would have been interesting to listen in on what the angels were saying during the ascension of Jesus Christ. They had to be scratching their heads, asking, "What in the world is the Lord doing!?" It appeared that Jesus was cutting His disciples loose, and the future of humanity hung in the balance. The Church would rise or fall with the handful of people squinting into the skies watching Christ disappear from sight. It wasn't quite that graphic, actually. First of all, Pentecost was on the way; the Holy Spirit of God was about to descend in a way that He never had before in all of history. And second, Christ was leaving them with a model and a structure of leadership that He Himself had lived for (and died for). Now He was passing on that structure to those who believed in His name.

Having accurate leadership structure is the only way for a church to go to the next level. What does accurate structure look like? What is the process of transition? How do you take a 50-plus-year-old church to health and growth? These are some of the most important questions the local church needs to answer today. But they don't need to just answer that question; they need to *understand* it.

The word *understand* means "submitting to what was stated." It's not just grasping a mental concept, it's responding to truth with obedience. To understand means "to stand under" — that's the literal meaning. It means to place yourself underneath an appropriate authority in an appropriate way. This type of understanding is essential to any church that aspires to great VALUE Vision, Attitude, and Leadership are always essential. But they find their power when they are manifested in a church structure based on biblical understanding. If you want to see the rural church grow and have a relevant impact on its community, it is imperative to have the right structure! The right structure is the sizzle on the steak, it's the tracks for the train, it's the oxygen for the fire, the steam for the engine, the . . . well, you get the idea.

Standing Under God

There is a pledge that our country used to say that mentioned something about being "one nation, under God." It meant something back then, but I'm afraid that we've lost it, and something different has taken its place. The unchanging words of Scripture, however, have not allowed that concept to fade.

Romans 13 makes it clear that all authority originates with God and, therefore, everything, everyone, everywhere is "under God." The centurion who came to Christ, begging for the healing of his paralyzed servant, knew what this meant as well. "I myself am a man under authority, with soldiers under me." He understood the God-given authority in Christ, and he stood under it in his time of need (Matt. 8:9). We find this amazing structure of leadership from Genesis to Revelation. But perhaps none are quite as piercing as the one we read about in Matthew 28:18–20:

> Then Jesus came to them and said, "All authority in heaven and on earth has been given to me. Therefore go and make disciples of all nations. . . ."

In this passage, Christ's authority and our mission are linked inseparably. We, under God, are to stand under the rock-solid structure that is Jesus Christ as we go about His mission.

Standing Under Scripture

Every Sunday, when I take to the platform and open my Bible, I am truly humbled that I have the privilege to dive into the perfect, flawless Word of God and bring out truth that is as relevant and real and as current as the morning newspaper . . . even more so! All Scripture is "God breathed." Unless you flunked out of Awana, you know that God's Word is profitable for teaching, for reproof, for correction, and for training in righteousness, so that servants of God might be equipped for every good work that God has prepared for us to walk in (2 Tim. 3:16–17).

Everybody agrees, right? Uh-huh. Then let me say this: if you go about your day saying, "I'm just going to cast off the Word today. I'm not going to discipline myself to dive into it. I don't really need it right now, maybe later" — if you say that, you are going to miss out on the anointing of your soul to act and to make right decisions. Once you've passed the Book aside, you will soon find yourself living a lie. The minute you say it's not relevant for every detail of my life, then the Bible becomes a fable and a fairy tale. Sure, it's nice and neat and we would never throw it in the trash, but when we say that we're not going to apply it, truth becomes subjective to my own personal theology or thought process.

Since we believe that we stand under the authority of Scripture, then, man, let's start acting that way! We need to be determined to teach and receive a relevant message from God, whether that means sitting at a restaurant or sitting in a small building with green pews and multi-colored green carpet that smells like just a tinge of rat urine and moth balls. We need to be taking that Word to the back roads, sharing the gospel message of the unchanging Word of God with passion, precision, and power that is sharper than any two-edged sword. That's where we begin to see a transformed life. When the Word of God transforms someone, he or she can't wait to tell someone else. In a small rural community, that transformation speaks loudly and the news about it travels quickly. I believe that electricity can move even faster in the rurals than it can in a metro area or a church of 1,000.

A lot of people ask why we continue to be Southern Baptist. (Let's be honest, we don't necessarily fit the stereotype.) I always answer, "Because doctrinally you just can't go wrong." Those guys believe the Word of God and stand under it. Not that I'm against non-denominational, but it's a fit for us because of our shared respect for the Bible. (If you're denominational, I really hope that you can say the same.) I think what we do at BNC is unique. A lot of churches might have the look or feel of BNC; it's the conservative Bible teaching that is causing the transformation.

Now, just a quick, extremely important question: if we take God's Word seriously in almost every other area of our personal and corporate lives, why in the world wouldn't we look to God's Word to understand His intended leadership structure for the church? Hmmm.

Standing Under a Shepherd (Pastor)

Is there anybody in this country who hasn't seen at least a portion of one of the 354 Rocky movies? It's pretty amazing that Sylvester Stallone came back after decades had passed and climbed back in the ring one more time as the Italian Stallion. But the thing is, he wasn't the original "Rocky." That role went to a fisherman named Peter, and Jesus is the one who gave it to him. Jesus looked at him and said, "You are Rocky, and upon this rock I will build my church, and the gates of hell will not prevail against it." (See Matt. 16:18.) Peter still had to walk through the valley of denial, but Jesus' words rang true. When the New Testament church was being established, it was Peter who was preaching in Acts 2. Sixteen times we are told how the Church grew in those early days, and Peter was at the helm the whole time. He was a pastor.

Then all this church planning and strategy stuff started to emerge. Throughout the 13 epistles, we see that Paul was the pastor of all these churches via the written word. I think it was by far the greatest example of multiplication through a "multi-campus" church that has ever been seen. In those early days, leaders didn't have the qualifications to bringing the Word of God alive, because all they had at the moment was the Old Testament. The New Testament was being inspired and penned as they grew through that multi-campus approach, relying on the written word coming through their pastor, Paul.

In Acts 6 we see the selection of the first team of deacons. Why? Like Moses, the early leaders were getting bogged down in necessary logistics of church life that were distracting them from study and prayer. Note that these servant-leaders (the *deakonos*) were selected by Paul because they were recognized as being "full of the Spirit and wisdom." As God continued to give the words of Scripture to these early apostles, His intended structure for the Church became more and more clear. The letters of First and Second Timothy, in particular, give very clear instructions to the leaders within this structure, with the requirements for selection and the qualifications clearly spelled out in 1 Timothy 3.

Please note: nowhere in these accounts or in these directives do we find a hint of the democratic process that forms the underlying structure of so many churches today. It's just not there. We find pastors leading, leaders selecting servant-leaders, and servant-leaders being equipped and mobilized for strategic mission. Period. It was a top-down structure that started with the authority of Christ, transferred by the Word of God, through pastors who mobilized and equipped servant-leaders, who matured to become pastors and mobilizers who did the same.

Somewhere along the line we fell into this "city council" approach of leading church. All of a sudden we get in the church and we feel like it is a popularity contest, where the masses, and not the leaders, are doing the actual leading, where the biggest mouths and the biggest wallets get heard the most. We get bogged down in the bureaucracy of democracy, rather than the precision and efficiency of a theocracy. We've fallen prey to the taxpayer system — or worse, we submit to the whims of the big-dollar donors who are keeping the lights on and paying to get the roof fixed. Let it be known that this leadership structure did not come from Scripture, it came from our culture, and it's very difficult (and impossible in most situations) to strategically pursue vision with the structure turned upside-down like that.

Repeatedly, Scripture uses the shepherd analogy to describe the role of the pastor. Pastors lead . . . at least that's what the Bible says they're *supposed* to do. Pastors are also like the coach of a football team. The coach is the one who is responsible for the game plan. He is the one who oversees the training and the workouts. He is the one who sends plays into the thick of the game as necessary. The team players on the field are often exceptionally gifted in what they do. They have strengths and abilities that the coach doesn't have. Oftentimes they have to make key decisions right on the spot under the understanding of the coach's overall game plan.

Are they brainless clones? Absolutely not. In the locker room and in the coach's office discussion is always open, feedback is welcomed, and opinions are valued. But in the huddle, there's no voting going on. In the huddle, the quarterback leads just like our campus pastors do. We have six other campuses, each with a pastor, and I don't know what they are doing minute-by-minute. Ultimately I know they have our vision and they are going to be an extension of me. I don't have to wonder what their answers are going to be because they understand the heartbeat of the church. I am so close to them personally that they know what I am thinking; they know what I would say; they know which direction I would go; they know which plays I would call. So our whole body, even at different locations, works together as one unit under one coach. It takes leadership to do that. The pastor is that central leader point that just has to be there.

I Know What You Are Thinking...

Something about this causes the hair to stand up on the back of your neck, doesn't it? This goes against the grain of nearly everything in Western society (except a privately owned business). We were raised on the virtues of "government for the people, by the people." Our forefathers shed their blood so there would not be taxation without representation. Yeah, democracy is one of our ingrained political values, and I'm not going to dispute it. What I am saying is that that is not the structure that God laid out for us through the Scriptures. We must be willing to stand under the authority of Scripture regardless of what kind of a political system we value. But nonetheless, let's take a quick look at some of the objections to a theocratic structure of leadership.

Control Freaks. This is a huge one. Throughout history we have seen men and women who have abused their power. Kings, dictators, megalomaniacs — all of them have used and abused their authority for personal gain. Pastors are not above this. Control freaks will cause power struggles and will manipulate, cause conflict, and be domineering *no matter what structure you are under.* If your pastor is a control freak, it's not going to work no matter what. I have found over and over that power struggles emerge out of insecurity and fear. In those situations you have a God problem and not a structure problem, because God leaves no room for this type of behavior in a pastor-led structure. Consider this charge by Peter:

> Be shepherds of God's flock that is under your care, serving as overseers — not because you must, but because you are willing, as God want you to be; not greedy for money, but eager to serve; not lording it over those entrusted to you, but being examples to the flock (1 Pet. 5:2–3).

And again, Paul's words are so strong in Philippians 2: *we are to take on the attitude of Christ,* humbling ourselves and becoming obedient to death. *That's* the biblical structure. Without that attitude it really doesn't matter what structure you have.

But let's be honest, control freaks are a big problem in democratically run congregations, as well. There are many glowing exceptions, but a lot of deacons are power hungry. They think that if they get on the board they are the bosses over everybody else, including the pastor. The problem is that most of them don't know jack squat about the church and they certainly aren't giving their life for it. They want all of the control with none of the responsibility. If the church is going great, it is their success. If the church sucks, they fire the pastor. This was so obvious back in our church's history when the deacons voted down adding sand to make a volleyball court for outreach to kids. The people making that decision didn't have the passion to reach the people and probably hadn't led anyone to Jesus in 30 years . . . if ever. Not all, but so many deacon committees running rural churches don't know jack about ecclesiology or theology, yet we give them the power to decide what takes place in reaching a lost world for Christ? That's not the biblical role of a deacon at all. They are to be passing out bread to the hungry, not serving the Lord's Supper only to the spiritually fat.

Loose Cannons. Okay, this next objection sounds like this: if our church becomes pastor-led, what stops the guy from going nuts on us? Where is his accountability, and who keeps him in check when it comes to finances, theology, his personal life, etc.? Who's to say he doesn't turn into a loose cannon blasting away at anything he desires?

Good question. The answer is: a good system of checks and balances. Accountability in our structure comes through the established elders/staff/pastors (whatever you want to call them) as well as through our denomination. If you decide to go the direction of biblical leadership, you'll want to make sure you have safeguards built into your system as well. For example, we have a trustee team that deals with all the finances. I don't even look at the finances. I don't know who tithes how much because I don't want big givers to think they can sway me. No offense, but the statistics show that wealthy Christians give away a much smaller percentage of their income than those from more modest incomes anyway. Again, I know there are exceptions, but that doesn't impress me. I'm not going to try to kiss up to him and stick my nose where I shouldn't. I'm going to be constantly focused on my calling, and that is shepherding.

Again, if your pastor goes off on you like a loose cannon, you haven't got a man of God in the first place. When a pastor is leading effectively, he has everything in the house in order. You see it in his kids and his wife. He is humbly sharing his weaknesses in front of the people that he loves the most. You see accountability with his staff and with his peers.

And if it gets really bad, in our bylaws at least, I can always be fired.

Blind Guides. A third objection is a little bit harder to articulate, but it all comes back to the same problem of a lack of vision. Many congregants are resistant to the idea of following their pastor because they don't know where the pastor is going, he shows little more than milquetoast passion for the mission, and he lacks the leadership attributes to direct the body in a meaningful direction.

Do I have an answer to this? No. Many pastors do not have vision because they do not listen to God's plan for them, or it is simply not within their abilities and gifts. They are spending the majority of their time studying God's Word for a message. They are spending the rest of the time putting out fires instead of starting them. And on top of that, they're spending all their time hoping no one sees what is really going on in their personal lives and in their families.

Lack of vision is a huge problem. A visionless pastor in a pastor-led structure is not much better than a visionless pastor in a congregationally dominated structure. A pastor with vision in a democratic structure can still make it work, but it's going to be like wading through the mud much of the time. Transforming committees into teams and keeping the vision continually in front of the congregation will allow the church to move ahead, but it's really cumbersome and takes a lot of extra work, and sometimes it just won't work at all.

But when you have a visionary pastor working through a biblical structure, when the accountability is in place, when the teams are developed, when the leadership is emerging, and the attitude is correct . . . when all the pieces are in place, hang on!

Action Points

Okay. If you're still with me, then let me lay down some applications. I'm assuming that if you've made it this far through this book, you're serious about growing a rural church. I'm assuming that you realize the growth doesn't happen without change and without conflict, even if that conflict is within yourself. If you are on board with that, then great, because true transformation requires true dedication and determined action:

> ✍ **If you are a pastor and you don't have vision, either get vision or step aside with grace and dignity.** Are you simply not a visionary? Calmly step aside and let someone else take that set of reins. Are you a

good teacher like most pastors are? You've probably got plenty of other passions that have been sidelined because you are trying to lead. Exercise those gifts to the fullest and be free to do what you do best.

If you are a leader (someone who is resisting the urge to settle) then stand under your pastor. He needs the support; you need to pick him up. Find out what he needs. If it has nothing to do with what you are good at, do it anyway. Everyone in rural America is a chameleon anyway; that's part of our strength, that's how we survive. We are farmers, fathers, ranchers, mechanics, cooks, and accountants . . . if there's a problem, we will figure something out. If there's a need, we get it done. And I'm telling you, your pastor needs you. Even if you're wrestling with the church structure issue, get over it; get under it and go for it.

If you are bogged down in a bureaucratic democracy, change it now. I think it's one of the most important commitments you can make to the growth of the Church. I have a dear friend who has a child who will never grow to more than three feet. His skeletal system will not allow him to grow because of an inherent deficiency in his bone structure. They are going to love him and do everything they can, of course, but yeah, they know this child is terminally ill. If you love your church, you will do the same, no matter what structure you end up with. But please understand: you have the option before you to do the surgery to remedy what ails your congregation. It might be a real fight to get them onto the operating table. You better decide ahead of time that you're willing to go to the wall and back. But I'm telling you, it's worth it. The process is not complicated; all you need is the determination to walk it step by step.

1. Initiate. In order to start the process, I went to the deacons and told them that we wanted to do some investigating to find the most effective leadership structures possible. I told them I wanted to check out the bylaws and constitutions of the churches that were making things happen in order to find out how they were doing it. They were all for it. So I selected a handful of people I knew were on track with the vision for our church and we went to work. Transformation must be initiated.

Steps to Transformation

1 Initiate
2 Research
3 Write
4 Educate
5 Decide
6 Hang on

2. Research. We started with the Bible and let the Word of God show us how the early church was structured and what the New Testament clearly said about leadership responsibilities and leadership structure.

Then we started investigating the bylaws of numerous congregations[1]. This included churches from within our denomination and churches from other denominations; churches with pastor-led structure and congregationally led structure; churches that were growing like crazy (we didn't bother to look at churches that were dead or dying).

The most revealing insights came when I researched seven of the top fastest-growing churches in America from many different denominations. One of them had seven sentences in their entire bylaw structure! Another had dozens of pages, but we started to see some patterns and started to collect what we thought were the best ideas.

3. Write. We started by cutting and pasting. We continued to study hard and read a bunch more. As we did, we continued collecting what we felt were the strongest elements from

---

1   You can collect these bylaws on your own, if you want to. Most churches have them on their websites. But if it saves you some time, we have assembled a large, categorized cross-section of bylaws that you can download at www.BreakingAllTheRurals.com.

different sets of bylaws. Then we began to hone the document to personalize it for our church.

We outlined the role of the senior pastor, the campus pastors, the staff, and the servant-leaders. For example, the only thing that I can't delegate as a pastor is my responsibility to preach God's Word and my call to cast a vision. I have to be the one shucking the corn in these areas. Some pastors can choose to delegate some or even all of their teaching, but in my opinion the role of casting vision must always reside with the pastor. The pastor does the shepherding. Shepherds lead. In order to lead you have to know where you're going. And in order to know where you're going you have to have vision. The day you delegate vision is the day you relinquish your title as "pastor."

We included four things that are still up for congregational vote: If you want to see the details of some of the variables that we chose for our church, our bylaws and constitution can be downloaded online as well. We pulled that thing

Four Things Up for a Vote

1 The hiring and firing of the senior pastor. If I ever get taken out, for any reason, my staff would immediately take over, and the trustees would immediately start the process of hiring someone else.

2 The selling or purchasing of land. We felt like this was an important check and balance.

3 The selection and voting of trustees.

4 The annual budget. We think it's important to have an "open book" when it comes to our finances, as well as allowing the congregation a broad say in how their money is spent. When it comes to actual purchases within a category, the people responsible for an area have control. So we get both accountability and freedom. Works good for us.

together in about six weeks. When the deacons read it, they said, "Oh, this is good!" So we decided to take it to the congregation.

4. **Educate.** We did everything according to current bylaws, according to *Robert's Rules of Order* . . . but nothing more. We made copies of the bylaws and handed them out without fanfare and just sat and waited while the 30-day waiting period passed by. A couple of days before the monthly business meeting, a few people started reading it and brought up some objections, but basically, we just kind of slid the thing through.

You might decide to take a whole different approach, but whatever you do, do not violate the decision-making rules of your current structure in order to push through a new one. That's just a recipe for disaster. Also keep this in mind: most churches have never been educated about how democracy can be totally crippling us from being able to stride and build God's kingdom at an exponential rate. By taking the time to explain the biblical structure and the tremendous advantages in it, and thoroughly answering the standard objections, you can really help the congregation make an informed choice.

5. **Decide.** I know guys who say you cannot turn an old institution. If you are running 1,000, you are probably correct, but if you have 50 people and you are ready to institute this, it can happen. Our vote was about 100 yes to 4 no. But remember, it's possible that you'll get to the end of this process and actually lose. That can be a real defining moment, because if you have done your research and you're educating thoroughly, the congregation is making a conscious decision between God's Word and the world, between Christ and our culture. If your congregation chooses the latter, you'll have some choices to make of your own. *Do I stay or do I go?*

6. **Hang on.** I don't think it was coincidence that our church went through some major battles at the same time we were

implementing a biblically based structure. If this was a step in the right direction — and I am so convinced that it was — we should have expected that opposition would come on all fronts. With this new structure intact, however, it's almost as if the church took on a new life as we surged forward, driven by our vision and unencumbered by the bureaucracy. All we could do was just hang on for the ride that started during that season, and has been blazing forward ever since.

Sure, I believe that God is sovereign. There isn't anything He can't do. All I know is that He really began to do it when we got things right and began to stand under a rock-solid structure. From that point on, it was clear that we were all standing under God, that we were standing under Scripture, that we were standing under the pastor. From my perspective as the senior pastor, it's been a tremendously humbling experience. It drives me to my knees when I turn around and see a staff, teams of servant-leaders, and a small army of volunteers who are dying to their own agendas, leaving behind their personal causes, and with creative passion and loyalty working as a body for a common vision. And I can't see how this ever would have happened without "understanding."

8
ENDURANCE

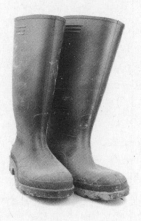

Enduring Excellence:
Well Done without Much

His master replied, "Well done, good and faithful servant! You have been faithful with a few things; I will put you in charge of many things. Come and share your master's happiness!" (Matt. 25:21, emphasis added).

We've really got only one shot. One life. One chance to make it count for eternity. Without that understanding, the decisions we make will make little sense in a temporary world. Back in the early days, it was always kind of weird when friends and family would come from the city to visit, particularly those who were familiar with the kinds of churches I had worked in before. I would show them around and they would nod their heads, but they always had this kind of awkward smile — like a sister who has gone to visit her brother in a mental institution for the first time.

Visiting from the outside, they just didn't get it. But the more I was on the inside, the more I understood. The more I understood, the more conviction and passion I felt for what God was doing around us and within us in Arkansas. It was something real; it was something valuable. It was so much deeper than the superficial appearances that are usually used to gauge success. And I was so thankful for it. If people raised eyebrows at the appearance of our building, so be it. Outward appearances of what a man can build miss the beauty of the land, the rhythm of the seasons, the power of the land, and the incredible potential that God has put inside the people who call these lands their home.

We were learning, and we were struggling, and we were breaking the rules about the rurals and replacing them with some rules of our own:

Four New Rules about Rural

1   Small doesn't have to mean boring.

2   Rural doesn't have to mean a lack of innovation.

3   Excellence is not found in the detail or design of a building.

4   Success is not found in the building's size.

We were also learning about *excellence* and *endurance,*
two of the most important concepts for building a rural
Christian community. Yes, we had vision, attitude, leadership,
and understanding, but the frosting on the cake was the
enduring excellence that greased the gears in everything we did.
Excellence and endurance got us through the day, and they let
us collapse in bed exhausted, knowing that we had taken that
one shot for eternity to the best of our ability and resources.

I'm convinced that God doesn't want average. He doesn't
settle for so-so. He isn't looking to build on just getting by.
He wants and expects our very best as leaders, pastors, and
congregations. And we need that, too. There's something about
the satisfaction that comes with giving your all that cannot be
duplicated by any other thing.

There are several environments that must be a part of any
church, rural or urban: great worship through song, aesthetics,
investing in life after life, a great marriage among staff, great
parenting among staff, relevant Bible teaching, practical
Bible teaching, momentum instead of movement, intentional
creativity, loyal staff, and, most critical of all, Vision, Vision,
Vision. Vision is what drives the "enduring excellence" that can
become the branding of the rural church.

*Are you ready to "Make the Change"? We
began with simple ideas to start achieving
with excellence; learn more in this short
video at* **www.nlpg.com/bnc.**

Excellence in Mission

Before jumping into this section, it's important that we
establish yet another new rule: vision can be pursued and
mission can be done well without much. How do you raise
the money necessary to grow a church in a blue-collar area? By
learning to produce excellence with a barbwire budget. How

can you enable a team with little to no resources to grow and go with BIG ministry? Through commitment to endurance.

Listen, every growing church has the same struggles with finances. That's just part of the territory. When God is pushing vision forward, the resources usually follow; they don't go before us. We need to be willing to step out in faith — to begin to wade out into the sea before the waters part. When it comes to finances, it is all dependent upon vision and call. It's the same in churches of any size, just not with the same number of zeros on the end! What if you had an extra $100, $1,000, $10,000, $100,000, or $1,000,000? Prayerfully, you wouldn't do any-thing differently, because God-given vision is not dependent on finances. His work, done His way, will never lack His supply. Far too often a lack of finances is used as an excuse to do things with mediocrity and shortsightedness. Because the coffers aren't overflowing, we settle for second best, or third, or fourth, or something that doesn't resemble the best of anything at all. When we erase that barrier from our thinking, we learn how to be creative, responsible, and tremendously resourceful with what we have here and now.

BNC held services in a local school gymnasium

I am willing to burn the candle at both ends for the cause of Christ. That's the way we started, and that's still our mode of operation. *Let's see what can happen with what we have,* I thought. We jumped in headfirst, willing to use whatever resources God provided to fulfill the mission He has given the church. Just don't jump in expecting an easy swim. Being a pastor at a rural church won't make you rich, and I will be honest, sometimes you will struggle to make ends meet. But there are creative, no-cost ways of fulfilling your mission with excellence.

I'm telling you that excellence and endurance is a mind set. It's part of the essential attitude that we must bring into ministry in the rurals. Whether it is our speaking, our messages, or our personal evangelism, if we are called, then we are called to make it good and make it sharp. There's no excuse for a presentation that is dull and dry. Yeah, it's a little bit easier for me now than it used to be. Now I have this team of incredibly gifted people who inject our website, worship services, and anything else that we do with professional, powerful audio and visuals. But that's not how we started. We started with two microphones, a deaf organ player, a sound guy who snoozed through the service, and overhead fluorescent lights all on one circuit. Even then, we were thinking "Can we add something; can someone play the trumpet, just anything to bring a fresh approach to it?" That was the attitude. *Whatever we do, it needs to be relevant; it needs to be transforming; it needs to make a difference in the community.* People don't want to just go to church anymore; they want to make a difference, and rural America is the same way.

"Rural" means "traditional" too often. There are those huge eclectic church buildings sitting empty over in Amsterdam and Denmark because they didn't have the vision to grow the ministry — they became immobilized in their traditions instead. Like a herd of woolly mammoths, they got stuck in tar pits of their own making. Refuse that! If you're going to go rural, you need to think like a missionary. Forget what you learned in seminary and learn to think outside the box, always looking for new and innovative ways to share God's love and His message of salvation. Missionaries are educated to do whatever it takes to get the job done. I once talked to a missionary who was going to a small village of about 30 people in Senegal. He had amazingly creative ideas, such as delivering bread wrapped in paper with the gospel message about Christ being the bread of life printed upon it. Maybe it worked, maybe it didn't, but this guy was thinking creatively and outside of the box with resources that he had in hand. Around the world, indigenous people groups are being reached in this way. Why not reach rural America with the same type of creativity! Rural America needs to see things done excellently.

I know they say, "If it ain't broke, don't fix it." I'm learning to say, "If it ain't broke, you might need to bust it!" Hey, if you don't want things to change, then just keep doing everything exactly the same. If you want to turn up the heat, you need to do it with excellence. You need to shake things up a little bit in any way that makes things better. I can hear you saying it right now: "My people are not into looks, lights, and fancy stuff on stage." You are right — until they see it done right once. Train them to desire excellence and God will be glorified. If your bulletin is still halfway produced, your children's area smells like mildew, your student area has a broken foosball and ping-pong table, your lobby smells stale, then your standard is not excellence. Excellence does not cost a lot of money: it costs in time and vision.

There are so many things like this you can do on zero. If we can do it, anyone can do it. When I came to South Lead Hill, the church's annual budget was around $40,000, and that included a salary and benefits for me and my family of six. I'm telling you, God can do it. He's in the business of feeding thousands with a couple of fish and a few loaves of bread. He knows how to stop the sun in the sky and give you a couple extra hours to fight. He knows that the widow gave more with her mite than all the other big-time donors gave through their endowments. My friends, we simply have to get thinking outside the box or we're going to get so claustrophobic and so self-focused that we shrivel up and die no matter what.

Let's take international missions, for example. Because of financial constraints, most churches, both rural and urban, give only token involvement to reaching the lost nations of the world. "After we grow we will give" is the general mentality. The problem is that missions only get the leftovers (and of course, the way things are, there's almost never, ever any leftovers). But you know what? If you're willing to think outside of the box and network with other innovators, you and your church can have an immediate personal impact on the world by touching the lives of speakers from around the globe — and you can do it starting today. (Not tomorrow, *today!*) We will talk about how your church can begin its own worldwide ministry in the next chapter, but there's no need to wait, because ministries such as Global Media Outreach (GMO) can get you started with a few clicks of the computer mouse.

There's nothing magical about this, just applied technology. GMO has created hundreds of websites that are giving answers to the questions that people around the world are asking. Seekers from every country on the globe are responding:

> I'm 32 and I've never been so lost in my life. I just want to give up and die; the only thing that keeps me going is my seven-year-old son. I need help. I do not know how to start or what to do. — Woman in Nice, France

> I am Muslim but I want to be Christian, so which kind of help will you do? I'm thinking about myself after the changing of my religion. I have become tired from this area's situation and all the day they pass their time; like in suicide attack. — Man in Pakistan

About 20 percent of those who come to the websites indicate some sort of a decision for Christ. You can actually watch this happen in real time at www.GMOEarth.com. A large percentage of those seekers request personal follow-up through e-mail. Throngs of people are visiting GMO websites each year, with tens of millions indicating decisions for Christ, and hundreds of thousands ending up in e-mail relationships. But here's the clincher: *there aren't nearly enough people to follow up on those who want more information about the gospel or just want to e-mail someone about Christianity.* Global Media Outreach can connect you and your church to do just that! With a few clicks of the mouse, they can train you and then start connecting you with people from Madagascar, Thailand, Indonesia, Latvia . . . *and it doesn't cost a dime.* Contact GlobalMediaOutreach.com to get connected today. Why not?!

I'm convinced that there are hundreds and thousands of innovations like this just waiting to be discovered by the rural church. In fact, our lack of material and financial resources is probably to our advantage, forcing us to come up with new and highly strategic ways to minister in our communities and our world. If we weren't forced to innovate, we would probably just settle for "the way we've always done it before."

Great aesthetics at BNC come at little to no cost.

Shannon with backdrops for the "Elation" series

Encouraging character in the BNC Kids area.

Excellence in Aesthetics

Most people look at the outward appearances of a facility to get their first impression of an organization. But that's too bad, because what's going on inside isn't necessarily reflected on the outside. How many huge structures are housing dead, lifeless organizations? How many bare-bones facilities are bursting at the seams with life and vision? For the first two and a half years, we held the course in our original church buildings, creatively allocating the limited resources at our disposal. Which brings me to a very simple point: it doesn't really matter what building you are in; your church can grow if it has vision, attitude, leadership, and understanding. If your environment shows excellence in its aesthetics, that's all the better. But let's get this straight: the church is not a building. It never was, and it never will be. The churches are a congregation made up of Christ-seeking congregants, and the church is exploding in parts of the world where physical buildings are non-existent. But this is not an excuse to be poor stewards of the facilities that we do have. Our facilities are a reflection of our vision and our mission, and we need to treat them and display them with excellence — even if we have to do it with very little.

We went out and found out how much a gallon of paint cost and we started painting. We started freshening up; we started burning candles; we started doing anything we could so that those first sensory elements in a human being were satisfied when they walked into the building.

We started sprucing up the children's area at no cost by asking the church to donate some of their clean toys. That was a critical need because in about six months, we went from one kid to about ten in the preschool and nursery area. For adults and teens, we tried rearranging chairs, changing light bulbs, putting up new but inexpensive decorations. We did just about anything you can imagine to make the place feel, look, sound, and smell great. Some things we changed just for the sake of change — symbolic alterations that showed we weren't anchored to predictability.

Finding ways to make things excellent and still cut costs is so easy, unless you are too lazy to stretch yourself. Many times we just spend because we have a budget for it instead of creating out of what we have, and I think the results are often far less excellent. We changed our stage appearance regularly on a no-cost budget. We created a winter wonderland in the lobby one Christmas — all thanks to borrowed live trees put into containers. And then thanks to some other borrowed stuff, we created a log cabin interior on the stage. It was welcoming and an awesome setting for preaching our holiday message, *Gifted*. For another series called *Custom Conversion,* we got vintage car owners to lend us a few vehicles that were on the stage for a month. Would anyone have imagined that if they didn't *have* to?

Creatively improving aesthetics is an awesome place to unleash volunteer energy in your church, particularly if you don't have many resources to work with. Give them the vision. Teach them to dream big, and then stand back and look out. You will be amazed at how well things can be done without much.

Time to Build?

I was so locked into my own idea of growth when we started this gig that I couldn't imagine the opportunities God would reveal through our need. I had always equated big ministry with big buildings. If God had given us that right off the bat through our first planned building project, I don't think we ever would have discovered what He really wanted us to do. Going big doesn't have to mean building a new building. Therefore, there are at least four strategically important questions to ask before you plan to break ground:

1. **Do we** *really* **need a new building?** Don't assume that you do. God can provide what you need through other sources (like He did with the donated building from Elixir Baptist). He might be leading you to multiply yourselves through multi-sites rather than just growing in one location. There's nothing wrong with building, but it's not necessarily the best! Think it through and make sure that you're not giving in to Christian peer pressure or pride to build bigger and better.

   If you sincerely pray about this and the answer comes back yes, then you'll have a few other questions to answer.

2. **Do we need a capital fundraising team?** I highly recommend a fundraising team such as The Gage Group or Charis Group to help you. If you do not have the resources for this kind of help, be certain to network with pastors and church leaders who have gone through the fundraising process. Remember: people don't give to need, they give to vision. Cast vision for excellence and your church will respond financially. Share the vision you have, give them a taste of it, and watch them respond.

3. **Does our plan maximize "usable" space?** Don't build stuff you don't need! So many churches have the majority of their square footage committed to rooms instead of space.

Our philosophy in building was to create space that could chameleon into whatever we needed. So many churches spend too much time on areas that the unchurched or first-time visitor will never grace, such as Sunday school space, fellowship halls, and administration areas. Prioritize your worship area, children's area, and lobby area. Prioritize "sight and light" in your design. God said, "Let there be light," and created not just the sun but stars, rainbows, the moon, and more. Be very intentional about how your facility sounds as well. People are drawn to great sounds: waterfalls, wind, rain, birds chirping, kids giggling, waves, and more. Have great sound in your auditorium and also in your education areas. And don't forget about intentional aromas. Good smells are a draw: coffee brewing, bread baking, honeysuckle, and the air after a rain. If you're going to build, build with excellence, catering to the eyes and ears and nose of all who will enter.

4. **Who is on the building team (committee)?** Do not, again I say, *do not* have a large team. Do not vote on everything. Do not allow someone other than the senior pastor to direct this team. And don't memorialize anything! Do not let the church vote this team into being, but hand select each member.

5. **Who am I building this for?** Build your facility with environments in mind to reach the unchurched, not just keep the big givers. Make it highly functional for your existing body, but consider making it available for community use, too. Our primary and sole purpose is to build so that God's glory might be revealed.

Bare Bones Brainstorming

Listen, I've gotten to the point where I believe that excellence is not only the essential goal of the rural church, but also that excellence has little, if anything, to do with finances.

By far the most powerful tools at our disposal are not linked to the budget. Consider these things that can be done really cheap with great excellence:

1. Outreach: it costs very little to lead someone to Jesus.

2. Add volunteer staff: the pews are filled with those waiting for a visionary service project.

3. Object lessons during your teaching: props and illustrations are usually free. (I just bought a piece of Plexiglas and screwed it to some muffler pipe, making a cool teaching board.)

4. Prepare your messages in advance ('nough said!).

5. Community groups: curriculum can be produced from your weekend teaching notes and e-mailed for nothing.

6. Set design: planning your teaching in advance allows you time to find paint, boards, fabric, and lighting to create a wonderful environment for your worship/teaching experience.

7. Pray!

8. Student ministry: Most student ministry can be funded on zero. I did not say all, but most can be funded with the help of volunteers and creativity. Our Wednesday night services operate on a zero budget, and we have hundreds attend weekly.

9. Staff: Many positions in your church can be lead effectively by volunteers. One area where you should never have a volunteer is in your finance office — NEVER! Look for the leaders just waiting to go to the next level in your organization.

10. Administrative office space: Some of our staff does not

have office space at the church, but we are all connected
by the Internet. We built office space at one campus from
volunteer labor and materials.

The list could go on and on. I'm convinced that this is
one of the keys to growth, innovation on a shoestring budget.
Check out what other people are doing with little or nothing.
Share your latest attempts to do well without much at www.
BreakingAllTheRurals.com, and you will bless others seeking
ideas and inspiration to do the same.

Endurance

Simply defined, endurance is excellence over the long haul.
Excellence doesn't come easily and it has to be teamed with
endurance. Ministry in any location is a challenge — both
for yourself and for your family. Rural ministry is even more
challenging because out here you cannot hide or fake your way
through the message. People see you living your life and your
faith daily. You are held to very high standards — and you
will be a target of other Christians as they judge you on your
ministry and your work in the community. Yeah — you better
be ready to endure plenty!

I believe that endurance is a lost character quality in our
world. Endurance is crashing through the breaking points!
When we break through, then God's glory shines through;
when we give up, God's glory is put up! What is God calling
you to endure?

- A frustrating relationship
- A tough job
- A cantankerous committee
- A financial struggle
- A diet and exercise
- A wayward child or maybe just spiritual discipline

God has plenty to say about endurance — whether you are a pastor, church volunteer, or congregant. He has plenty to say to that tired, worn-out, burned-out, still in-the-trenches soul of yours. There isn't a one of us that doesn't need rest, reflection, and truth. Nothing supplies that like time in prayer with the Word of God. Nothing. We don't find the inner strength by pulling ourselves up by our bootstraps or listening to the latest motivational message. True strength comes at the feet of Jesus, in a quiet place, where we can let the truth of God's Word resonate in the soul, weary as it may be. Wherever you are right now, no matter what you're facing, rest in Him and let His words speak to you now; let truth saturate not only your mind, but your heart as well.

> For everything that was written in the past was written to teach us, so that through endurance and the encouragement of the Scriptures we might have hope (Rom. 15:4).

> May the God who gives endurance and encouragement give you a spirit of unity among yourselves as you follow Christ Jesus (Rom. 15:5).

> Rather, as servants of God we commend ourselves in every way: in great endurance; in troubles, hardships and distresses (2 Cor. 6:4).

> Being strengthened with all power according to his glorious might so that you may have great endurance and patience (Col. 1:11).

> We continually remember before our God and Father your work produced by faith, your labor prompted by love, and your endurance inspired by hope in our Lord Jesus Christ (1 Thess. 1:3).

> But you, man of God, flee from all this, and pursue righteousness, godliness, faith, love, endurance and gentleness (1 Tim. 6:11).

You, however, know all about my teaching, my way of life, my purpose, faith, patience, love, endurance (2 Tim. 3:10).

Teach the older men to be temperate, worthy of respect, self-controlled, and sound in faith, in love and in endurance (Titus 2:2).

I, John, your brother and companion in the suffering and kingdom and patient endurance that are ours in Jesus, was on the island of Patmos because of the word of God and the testimony of Jesus (Rev. 1:9).

If we are distressed, it is for your comfort and salvation; if we are comforted, it is for your comfort, which produces in you patient endurance of the same sufferings we suffer (2 Cor. 1:6).

From Genesis to Revelation, God takes endurance seriously. The Bible is filled with stories of endurance — personally and professionally and in terms of ministry. It's a big deal to God. You can't succeed without it. And when you are called into ministry — you need it. The pattern of "change, conflict, growth" will always be with us, and as we move forward for the Kingdom, our loving Father will allow difficulty to push us to our knees — for He is no stranger to pushing men and women to the edge of "self" where they realize that they have nothing left in and of themselves except broken, burned-out, and empty flesh. And that's just where He wants us; because that's where we stand with empty hands and open arms ready to receive again from Him, admitting our helplessness, submitting to His will, and trusting again in the power of His presence in our lives to do His work through us.

Truly, the pursuit of enduring excellence will bring us quickly to the end of our human abilities, where we find out that we are the vine and He is the branches, and apart from Him we truly can do nothing (John 15:5). Yes, excellence and endurance is one of our goals, one of the necessary aspects of VALUE that allows the rural church to grow.

So do not throw away your confidence; it will be richly rewarded. You need to persevere so that when you have done the will of God, you will receive what he has promised (Heb. 10:35–36).

Whatever you do, work at it with all your heart, as working for the Lord, not for men, since you know that you will receive an inheritance from the Lord as a reward. It is the Lord Christ you are serving (Col. 3:23–24).

But by the grace of God I am what I am, and his grace to me was not without effect. No, I worked harder than all of them — yet not I, but the grace of God that was with me (1 Cor. 15:10).

Dear Father make it so! Make us weak so that we might be strong; make us fools so that we might become wise; give us as little as necessary to prove that You can do anything. Lord, by Your grace, give us Your vision, Your attitude, Your leadership. Give us a willingness to stand under Your leadership, and by Your mercy, grant us enduring excellence to fulfill Your call in our lives. To the glory of Your Son, amen!

transforming church in RURAL AMERICA

breaking all the (Rurals

PART 3

THE NEW HORIZONS

I waited patiently for the LORD; he turned to me and heard my cry. He lifted me out of the slimy pit, out of the mud and mire; he set my feet on a rock and gave me a firm place to stand. He put a new song in my mouth, a hymn of praise to our God (Ps. 40:1–3).

9
SATELLITES

Multi-Sites and Satellites:
Rural Goes Virtual

Look at the nations and watch — and be utterly amazed. For I am going to do something in your days that you would not believe, even if you were told (Hab. 1:5).

The mass exodus from South Lead Hill after the pew wars was the hardest thing I had ever experienced in my life — partly just because of the shock of the whole thing. I had been largely oblivious to the size of the sacred cows that were grazing and fertilizing within those church walls. After my little inadvertent escapade of sacred cow tipping, the ensuing flash thunderstorm, and then the evacuation of most of the campus . . . man, I just hurt. I went home disillusioned, defensive, and wounded — and I just bawled. Those who left must have felt the same. I was ready to pack up and head out. And those who left were probably hoping that I would! I still believed that rural America was the greatest mission on earth, but this was not what I thought I had signed up for. I entered a brief but very serious season of reflection and reconsideration. You know what I'm talking about, 46 steps from the parsonage to my office — yeah, I counted. There was a time in my ministry when people loved me and brought me blackberry cobbler. Now the only thing they left was angry messages on the phone machine.

VALUE

V ision

A ttitude

L eadership

U nderstanding

E nduring Excellence

In the moment, I thought we were done. But we weren't. It was just the beginning. We had difficulty, pain, and tears — and I'm learning that those are the things that bring meaning to true hope. We can hope because, above all things, we have God, and on top of that we also have V.A.L.U.E.s.

Vision. Everything you and I embark on must be in line with the overall organizational vision of your church. Our vision is to *Worship Him, Walk with Him, and Welcome Others to Him.* That vision drives everything we do (even if it requires removing memorialized idols of decades past).

Attitude. Everyone and every event must have a Philippians 2:5 attitude — *your attitude should be the same as that of Christ Jesus.* This attitude contains energy. All leaders, volunteers, staff, and events must be filled with this attitude and energy. Nothing depletes the effectiveness of your vision more than a bad attitude. (Painful as it was, the pew-war exodus got rid of a lot of inconsistent attitude in our little body.)

Leadership. Leadership is brought and taught. In the home, in the church, and in our personal lives, the greatest leaders on our team were taught before they brought it. It is up to us as leaders to attract leaders. If you are struggling with attracting leaders, you must ask yourself if you are a leader. The old Chinese proverb says, "He who thinks he leadeth and has no one following is only taking a walk." (The congregants that remained had proven that they were willing to resist the urge to settle and move on with the vision — even if it required tremendous change.)

Understanding. Each event and leader must be supporting the senior pastor's vision. We stand under God, under His Word, under the pastor, and under the other leadership in the church. Loyalty and getting "under" the pastor's vision is the key to success for every leader and event within the church. (We had that now.)

Enduring Excellence. This costs you absolutely nothing! Excellence must be oozing from everything you do within the local church. Most rural churches smell, look, and sound like they are from another planet. Aesthetics are important to God. Aroma is important to God. God's ears are attentive to the sounds of excellence and obedience. You can do excellence on a zero budget. (By making a low-budget but highly strategic decision, we had upset the apple cart. But by pursuing excellence with endurance, we had planted the seeds of amazing growth.)

God's ways are not our ways. We seem to have to learn that over and over again, because what He does is so counterintuitive to our way of thinking; it's just the way that God works.

- He uses the foolish to confound the wise.

- He uses death to bring life.

- He uses ashes to create beauty.

- He makes us weak so that we might be strong.

And as He did with Gideon and his army, God is willing to seriously deplete your ranks in order to win the victory His way. God works in obscurity. He seems to like it best when the odds are stacked so far against us that there's no question about where the glory goes when good things happen. For our struggling little church in the middle of Nowhere, Arkansas, He nearly wiped out our congregation so that it could grow, so that we would realize that we were standing on the edge of a new horizon, a fresh sunrise. He was ready to do some things that I would have never believed were possible. But I didn't know that. All I had at that moment was a pile of rubble and the distant memories of what I thought He told me on the white couch: *Shannon, what if I want to use you to blaze a trail to pioneer a work in rural America? What if I want to use you to do that?*

Echoes of a Distant Call

Being called to ministry doesn't mean that you walked an aisle at church camp as a kid or teen. It doesn't mean that your grandma prayed over you and said, "I know you are going to be a pastor." When you are called, God picks you up and puts you where He wants you. It is undeniable. You can't run from it. It is like the drawing I felt toward my wife Cindy back when I was 19, when I thought I was falling in love. Time and distance couldn't dilute it. I didn't see her or talk to her for 18 months after we met, but by the time I saw her again at 21, it was undeniable. It was like this magnet, like the call of God.

When you are ready to take *anything* and *everything* necessary to get into people's lives, when you have to watch them blossom, when you thrive on life change in others, then you probably have the call to ministry. When you believe that you are willing to take on the enemies and all the junk that will be thrown your way, then you are probably called.

I didn't have to think about it very long. By God's grace, I knew that we were called. By God's mercy, we hung in there. I dried my tears and went back to fight another day, personally holding on to the promise that God gave me about pioneering and blazing a trail in rural America. I reclaimed and clung to the prayer in Psalm 86:11:

> Teach me your way, O Lord, and I will walk in your truth; give me an undivided heart, that I may fear your name.

God had made it clear that if I was willing to let Him do that *in* me, then He would prosper *through* me. But in that season, I was forced to redefine "prosperity" altogether, because what He was doing defied worldly definitions of "success" and "failure."

 *There are essential things you need to keep in mind when your ministry starts to prosper. Watch "Vision & the Bills" at* **www.nlpg. com/bnc** *as I share that finances may be a continuing challenge, but God's financial blessings are constant as well.*

Forfeiting the Numbers Game

The media is drawn to that which draws other people. The Church is the same way. As a society and as a Church, we gauge success by size. Great teachers and great leaders have big churches. We give special credibility and honor to a pastor of 20,000 or the one on television, or the one with the big shiny building with multiple staff and a $30 million budget. Yeah, that's success, and that's where we all want to be. But I am telling you, we have made the large church the glamorous opportunity in ministry, and we have lied to ourselves while we often fail to see the enormous potential in small churches in small communities.

So many of us get so upset at the way the media drives elections. We really don't like the thought that the candidate who gets the biggest audience is the one gets the most votes . . . and yet we do the same thing with the local church!

Don't give me that baloney. As leaders it so easy for us to say, "Oh, if I just had _____, then I would be happy and successful." But please get this: If you aren't committed, if you aren't sure of your own calling, if you are not daily drawing close to God and discovering your vision, it doesn't matter if you have a church of 20 or 20,000. You won't be impacting lives. If you aren't called to rural America, you are always going to dream of the church of 1,000 down the road or in a bigger city. Or you are always going to dream about Outback Steakhouse. (Instead, you are eating at Smokey Beans. You know what I'm talking about!)

The emergence of the mega-church in the last two decades hasn't helped us come up with the biblical definition of success, either. The stats say that 61 percent of churchgoing Americans attend churches running 60 or less. And yet we look at the churches that have grown into the thousands and think that that's the standard and should be the norm. That's just not going to be reality in rural America. We don't have the resources to build multi-million-dollar facilities. There are very few places that are going to have the numbers to support those large campuses in rural areas. And we need to put those numbers in perspective anyway. If a guy has 10,000 people coming to church in a city of millions, he's just barely scratching the surface. But if you're in a town of a couple thousand and you have a dozen or so servant-leaders? Man, I'm telling you, God can use that team to reach the vast majority of your community and county. And don't tell me that things can't grow, because with VALUE they can, if God wants to move that direction.

We have got to break the "bigger is better" rule. I had gotten sucked into that mentality before God started breaking the rules I had about the rural church. Here is what I believe now: *the smaller they are, the healthier they are, because that's where God likes to work. God works in obscurity.* If you are sitting back and saying to yourself, "I want to have great numbers and great facilities," you are missing it. That may or may not come in time, and I really doubt it will before you are totally reliant on God and His vision. Know also that anything alive grows; so do not excuse small-plateaued congregations as God's will. When you see the vision clearly, it won't matter what the numbers look like. As pastors, once we realize a mega-church can't happen in every small town, then we know we have to go out with God's best to encourage, inspire, and lead these smaller facilities in these communities to have the impact God desires them to have. But you must first love people. Because the moment you decide to grow a congregation before reaching congregants, you have lost God's heart for the church.

Growth doesn't mean you go from 31 to 2,000; it may mean going from 31 to 66.

Thomas Rainer had a great quote. I read it just the other day. It says, "We need to develop seminarians to grow churches from 6 to 25." I thought, *That is powerful.* I just heard that as God's call to rural. Heading this call requires servant-leaders with leather-tough skin who are willing to go to the backside of the desert and back to give their communities a chance to go to heaven. I think most churches are ready for that kind of leadership.

Moving On

Just before everything blew up in our face, God allowed me to be a part of one of those magical ministry moments that was a much-needed reminder of what our vision was, and why we were doing what we were doing. Just before we went to the south campus, a man showed up at the South Lead Hill service. After church he called me, told me he loved the service, and asked if we could meet together. A few days later we shook hands and sat down at Neighbors Mill. He said, "Shannon, man, I enjoyed the message. I just have some questions about church." He started sharing a little bit of his story. His marriage was over. He gave up on his wife. He was empty and everything was coming apart . . . and he was very tired of all of it. "I just don't know what to do," he said over the steam of his coffee. "I really am excited about the church and I was wondering, what are the membership dues?" I should have told him they were

$10,000 a month and that we accept major credit cards . . . but in all honesty, the question broke my heart. *This guy has a broken heart and a broken life and he believes that there are membership dues in a church!? He was born and raised in Boone County — a county with over 60 area churches. Dear God, help us.*

I said, "There are no dues. The most important and most valuable thing you can do for yourself and for your marriage is to meet Jesus, and that's free. Has there been a point in your life when you met Him?" He started bawling, so we walked outside of Neighbor's Mill, bowed our heads, and I got to introduce my new friend to my Friend. The following Wednesday we introduced his wife to Christ, too. That is how it happens. One changed life, one congregant after the next congregant after the next congregant.

So March 30, 2005, we opened up the South Campus in the building we had been given by Elixir Baptist, and we went to 300 just like that. The church was electrified. People couldn't believe it. We were three years and a month into it by now and it continued to grow. After the blow-up in South Lead Hill, we went from about 300 to 350 in just a matter of months and then just kept growing through the year, one life at a time. At the Christmas Eve service we had 400 or so packed into our little facility. Most importantly, our vision, volunteers, and servant leadership continued to grow. But there wasn't anything glamorous or spectacular about the church itself. We were doing some things that were a little bit more relevant on the worship end, but the rest of it was just heartfelt vision to fulfill the mission.

As that started happening God gave me a revelation in my dreams to move things to the community gymnasium. That was odd — it appeared to be a step in the wrong direction. Most growing churches can't wait to get out of the gym and into their own real building, but God was taking us backward so that we could move forward. (Obscurity again!) But there was a problem: the school board said no, and I couldn't argue with their reasons. Seven miles down the road from our

church in our little town is the national headquarters for the
Ku Klux Klan, ironically called "Soldiers of the Cross Bible
Camp." (Great PR for the Cross and the Bible, don't you
think?) Because they could not discriminate, the school knew
that if they opened the doors to us, they would have to be
willing to let in everyone, including the KKK. Because of that,
they had never given anyone permission to use the building.
But incredibly, they felt led to go the extra mile for us. They
rewrote the school's bylaws to require a staff person to facilitate
all events in the gym. Then they put in a clause to say that if
a staff person ever associated with an organization the school
didn't support, the bylaws could be changed at that time and
no one would be allowed to use the gym again. So we were
in! The word spread and the first week attendance jumped to
about 620. It was impossible, really. I think we were doing some
things right, but this was starting to borderline on revival, with
no explanation other than God's Spirit moving through the
community.

And in reality, we hadn't seen anything yet.

The Sticks in the Digital Age

Rural America doesn't look like it has changed much at all
since World War II. Sure, tractors are bigger and new model
pickups are parked in front of the barbershop, but other than
that, everything looks about the same on the surface. But it
isn't.

Rural America is being impacted by the same information
technology breakthroughs as the rest of the world. Cable news
is reaching us. The cinemas are reaching us. We are getting
PS3s and Xboxes, and playing Rock Band (this year at least —
next year we will be on to something else). Outsiders might be
fooled by our flannel shirts and gravel roads, but we are moving
along the same information highway as they are, particularly
as DSL becomes more and more widespread. We have GPS
in our tractors and check today's commodity prices on our

BlackBerrys. We are brilliant, hard working, and innovative. With baling wire and a high-speed modem there is nothing we can't do well . . . except church.

When it comes to spiritual things, for some reason we cling to a withering contentment to sit in uncomfortable chairs listening to dry monologues and out-of-tune pianos. In all honesty, I'm not quite sure why that is. But as we continued to see life after life changed, I firmly believed that modern technology could, and should, be the friend of the timeless gospel. Shoot, God used a donkey to speak truth — so don't tell me that today God couldn't use a sound system, a satellite, or a podcast! The fact is, no matter where we are positioned in America, technology has made our geography irrelevant. The prophecy of Habakkuk 1:5 is our reality:

> Look at the nations and watch — and be utterly amazed. For I am going to do something in your days that you would not believe, even if you were told.

Truly, these are unbelievable days. What can be accomplished with the click of your right index finger would have been *unthinkable* just a few decades ago, and the things we can do today will most likely be obsolete just a few years down the road. (So forgive me with a smile if the cutting-edge stuff I'm excited about today is old school by the time you read this!) The key is this: *We have access to instant audio and visual communication with the entire developed world.* All we need to do is learn to tap into it. E-mail, websites, blogs, forums, Twitter, Facebook, and other social networks can transform the mission of the Church in small towns by *exponentially* increasing opportunities to share, care, connect, and provide visionary leadership. Talk about viral marketing in a light second. I can share my heart in a second with hundreds from our church and church leaders concerning any issue — and that's just for starters! I can get my word out via technology at no cost and so can every other pastor in rural America. That resource alone — training and educating technologies — is amazing.

I was talking about this with a pastor friend when he said, "But most of the people in my church are 60 years old." I just shook my head. That's not a decent excuse for overlooking some of the most powerful tools for ministry the world has ever seen — so far. While things are expanding at light speed, the technology itself is becoming easier and easier to use. The fastest-growing age group on Facebook is over 60 years old. And it's only going to get better and cheaper." He said, "Well I'm not sure the ladies in my church could afford it."

I said, "Go to the college. They have computers lying there they will donate to a church. Let these people take them into their homes, set them up for them, get them connected."

I would start with a Facebook training discipleship class. Get the whole church together; bribe them with a potluck; bring your best blackberry cobbler and say, "I am going to train you how to use Facebook." If you really want to motivate them, show them how they can have instant communication with their grandkids. Do that and you'll have blessed them beyond measure. They will see more pictures of those grandkids in five minutes than they have seen in years. *Grandkids connecting with grandparents almost every day?* What a dream! That alone is a grandparent's fulfillment of Habakkuk 1:5. But guess what else you have — you now have 20 grandmas that listen to you via your status update every day and prayer warriors that can be mobilized quicker than minutemen of the Revolutionary War.

Please listen to me on this: leaders resist the urge to settle at home and in the Church and in their personal lives. They also resist the urge to settle for old technology. Don't be the leader that says, "I have a computer, but I don't know how to turn the thing on." That phrase is not cool anymore. It was in the '90s, but not today. I believe God wants us to be constant learners and users of instruments that can spread His truth. Learn how to text on your cell phone. Send out a verse a day to all your members, create a prayer chain and update it instantly via texting. The technology is there, and learning to apply it is not brain surgery or rocket science; applying technology is really just a matter of the will and finding a couple of teenagers to help you press the right buttons. When we started to apply technology to our vision, the world *literally* started to come to Brand New Church, and God sparked a movement in small towns all across North America that is just now starting to burn.

The Genesis of iCampus

Like most churches, we had developed a pretty good website to back up our two physical campuses. But then we started to dream about expanding that website and turning it into a *virtual* campus where people from around the world could attend our services and be a part of our ministry. The cost was less than $2,000 to begin this adventure. Get this: today (at the end of 2009) we have 1,100 people from 66 countries around the world regularly attending our services. These are not "visitors" to our website; these are people who are registered participants in our worship and teaching service. We are seeing lives changed every week, and we do it at virtually no cost.

Does that blow your mind? It does mine! Ministering and worshiping simultaneously in dozens of countries with thousands of people from a town of 407? Habakkuk 1:5 indeed!

As our virtual campus began to catch fire, we wondered what would happen if we made a sizable investment by buying space on Google that sends people to a website to hear the gospel. In 110 days we ministered to 24,412 people from 140 countries . . . without ever leaving town. Today our website and our iCampus are some of the most efficient, inexpensive, and effective modes of fulfilling our vision, and I know God is just getting started with this.

Think you are too small or too rural to be used by God in a huge way? Take a couple of minutes to watch "Believe God" at **www. nlpg.com/bnc.** *See how little gifts are transformed into amazing ways to impact both our community and even our world.*

Construction begins for new building at Bergman.

Going Multi-site

It didn't take long to realize that we were going to outgrow even the gymnasium. So finally we resurrected the plans for building our own facility. Thirteen months later we moved, stretched our legs a little bit, and settled in. I honestly believed it was the end of our growth. But God's vision refuses to be limited. We realized that with proper use of technology, we could multiply what we were doing in different physical locations, *if* we stayed fully committed to our vision, attitude, development of servant leadership, maintenance of a proper structure of understanding, and did it all with enduring excellence. Thirteen months and three weeks after moving into our new building, we ended up with five campuses.

Our second campus began in Mountain Home, Arkansas, with a population of 11,012. It started to grow. Then we went to Goshen, Arkansas, an area near Fayetteville and Springdale (population 980). People from this area were driving 75-plus miles one way to Bergman because they were so desperate in rural America to have relevant worship and relevant teaching.

We thought, *Let's give it a shot and plant a campus in their area.*
It got started in October 2007 with 15, and in less than a year
it had 100 people and is still growing. Without the satellite
technology and multi-campus structure, we would never
have had the opportunity to do this, and most importantly,
our growing congregants were now maturing into full-
fledged servant leaders and pastors who could maintain our
commitment to building congregants rather than congregations.
The same thing happened with Bryant, Arkansas, a town of
9,000. Skeptics said there is no way we could make it happen
in that area. The Bryant campus is now 18 months old and
growing. Hundreds attend the weekend experience, and they
have over 200 children and youth on Wednesdays.

It seems like we may have tapped into God's heart on this
one. This is what people seem to need; and God is giving it.
Leaders and other pastors often ask me a lot of questions about
the multi-site campuses, including the following:

1. **How did you know that it was time to start multi-site
   campuses?** The plan was never to go multi-site, but reaching
   rural America forced the issue rapidly. As God continued
   to bless BNC, we found that people were driving 50-plus
   miles to attend a healthy church. As larger groups from
   those areas attended, we began campuses. God has blessed
   these campuses beyond my wildest dreams, and in my heart
   I believe the greatest days of this growth are just beginning.

2. **What is the most important thing to know before
   launching?**
   Know you are called to multi-site.
   Know you are called to the area.
   Have the RIGHT campus pastor in place.
   Know where to begin strong and what areas must evolve.
   Know who is the target audience.

3. **What technology is the most effective for message
   presentation?** A multi-site church needs cohesion in order

to maintain unity. That requires the ability to present the same message and cast the same vision to every campus. How you do that? You have three options:

a. Web Streaming — a good option except in rural America because of unreliable signals and narrow bandwidth limitations, but this will change for the better in the next couple of years.

b. DVD — duplicating DVDs is rock solid.

c. Satellite — great way . . . it's live and rock solid.

Knowing why you do what you do is the key here. This is not something to attempt in order to just be cool or relevant. You need to be called to this because it's a lot of work. At the same time, don't limit God or His resources. Just believe in your method (and your tech director)!

Again, you need to think outside the box. I've had people tell me, "Well, a video venue cannot work in rural America — at least not in my area." I have gone to the other campuses and the members say, "Hey, we like watching you on video better!" Rural churches need to be absorbed and get great teaching; that's part of the glue that holds us together. But the cool thing is that if they don't like a particular worship style, they can create their own live worship experience and still be connected with the whole body.

This model has worked well for our first five campuses. Lots of pieces have to come together to make it work, but the essential, indispensable ingredient is the committed volunteers and servant leaders working under a campus pastor who maintains the vision. Together, they continue to build more leaders who can multiply and do the same thing. We could seriously see this thing spread across the whole country. That's not necessarily our goal, but there's nothing that I can see to stop that.

A used Hummer with satellite equipment
purchased by the multi-campus BNC

Satellite Churches … Literally

Satellite churches are typically understood to be smaller
gatherings that hover some distance away from a larger mother-
ship church. I always had a vision to do it satellite, but I wanted
to use a *real* satellite to make it happen. The idea is awesome.
You transmit a signal to a satellite. Then the satellite broadcasts
it over an entire continent. Just one problem: the price tag was
about half a million dollars for the service and the equipment
that we would need. That was way out of our range, so we
took it to prayer . . . and we took it to eBay. Lo and behold, we
found all the equipment we needed for about $120,000 plus
a few odds and ends. But the neatest thing was that all that
equipment was installed in the back of a bright red Hummer. I
mean, this thing is a beast. Chrome wheels, smoked windows,
killer stereo — definitely a sign from God that this was the
direction we should go. We can now send a satellite feed from
anywhere on the continent *to* anyplace we want. Once I even
preached on the impact of the culture on the Church from the

corner of Times Square in New York City. (Fun!)

But the most important part of this gizmo is what happens on the receiving end: for $205 (shipping included) we can get a receiver and a dish to any place in the country. *That means we now have endless opportunities to create satellite home churches in areas where the need for quality ministry is high and the options for a quality church experience are slim.* Grasp that.

We train the house host, provide children's material, and give free marketing materials to get the word out in the community. Our first satellite home church launched on Christmas Eve 2008 in Yates Center, Kansas (population: 1,376). Ever been to Yates Center? There is nothing there. Nothing. But we just plopped a dish up a pole there and now they are connected — almost as if we are all in the same room. Same thing happened in Sandy, Utah, where we have started a satellite house church with a little different edge on it. Sandy is a good-sized city, but being just 21 miles outside of Salt Lake City, it's an evangelical desert in its own right. Now, through satellite, the water of God's Word is flowing through a new channel.

We pay $325 an hour on our end for the airtime. Anyone with the dish can receive anything we broadcast for free — *anyone* from the top of Canada to the bottom of Mexico and anywhere in between . . . and as far out in the

Home Churches Can Participate In:

- Live worship
- Live teaching
- Live interaction through TokBox, a great online video conferencing tool for conversations and encouragement
- Live leadership training
- Live conferences

boonies as can be. It is a deal! It isn't that we feel like we have the niche on truth or want to corner the market on worship or anything like that. We're not about that at all. Many great teachers and much great worship can be found in every city on the continent; we aren't trying to build a monopoly.

But what we *are* trying to do is use this amazing God-given setup to come into a rural town, *any* rural town, and share the resources and pass on the servant leadership we have been blessed with. We are either going to burn the ozone up or make a huge impact in rural areas across the country, but we can do as many campuses as we want. We could have 10,000 satellite house churches with the same $325. In rural America, that is what they need. Almost everybody has a TV but not everyone has a relevant church experience they can physically attend — so we are blasting that experience to them and giving them real channels of feedback to connect back to us in real time.

Our expanding vision is to get as much great teaching, inspirational worship, training materials, and ministry tools as possible into rural areas. Satellite home churches and multi-site campuses are the way to do it. In beta test stage are "BNC Remotes," which are house churches on steroids in selected rural communities. We will lease a community building or school, advertise with great fervor, and go for eight weeks and see what God grows. Stay tuned on that one!

By doing what the rural church rarely has the resources to do, together we can free up pastors and leaders to do what they do best, *build congregants.* By networking together and continuing to share our ideas, concerns, prayers, and vision with like-minded people who are sensing that call to reach rural America, God can unleash the incredible potential that lies buried in the heartland and beyond.

Seriously, who would have dreamed that something like this could happen anywhere, let alone in the middle of the sticks? We just about lost it all over 50-year-old pews in a musty-smelling building. Today I have no idea what the limits are. Satellite technology is allowing us to plant campuses in all directions, with the Internet campus by far the most effective, bringing in 200–300 new congregants each week. The multi-site campus and satellite house church is a no-brainer for rural ministry where believers have been struggling in sparsely populated towns, geographically isolated from the rest of the Body of Christ.

Just so you know, it doesn't have to be that way anymore, not for anyone.

A Call to the Called

For centuries, the rural church has been isolated and insulated from the greater Body of Christ by the sheer realities of geography. Those days are gone. There's absolutely no reason that we can't be networking together as leaders — those who are resisting the urge to settle — by sharing resources, encouragement, wisdom, and vision. We don't have to do it alone anymore; together we can do so much more and do it so much better.

What could we (all the churches and congregations) accomplish in this world if we all worked together? Why do rural pastors struggle and often despair alone rather than reaching out to others with similar challenges? Why is there a spirit of competition and possessiveness in rural American churches rather than seeing one another as part of the same faith family?

Good questions. I believe the answer lies in a fresh call of God that is spreading across rural America. We would be fools to try to force something like that. We would also be idiots to deny it if it's happening. All I know for sure is that too often the rural leaders feel isolated — not really sure how to reach out to others for solutions and inspiration for growing their own ministry. I truly feel that Brand New Church has been called to serve rural pastors and churches. From home church discussions to multi-site strategizing, from staff development to upgrading

BNC's broadcasts through its iCampus reaches
around the globe

the worship experience, we can connect via satellite with you
and your team exclusively or you could come in via TokBox or
satellite and join us for weekly "Staff Advance" and leadership
training. We can share teaching notes, message outlines, Sunday
school materials, youth group resources, and logos. None of this
was ever ours to start with; it would be a great privilege to share
with all.

We know that we are a bit "out there" in a lot of ways.
Certainly we are not a fit with everybody, and we don't want
to team up with anybody who doesn't have a specific call from
God to work together. And unfortunately, there are others who
probably won't let their pride accept help or resources from
an outside source, who will say, "he is an arrogant punk to
think he has something we don't." Sorry about that. But quite
frankly, I've been accused of worse, and that's not what we're
up to. What we are about is networking and giving jumpstarts
to churches that are ready to move with a vision. You lose no
autonomy and no dollars except the repayment of the satellite
dish — if you can, and whenever you can.

Yeah, it has been a wild ride since the day we pulled the pews — the beginning of an incredible journey that I think is just getting started. These are new days, and God is on the move. Just know that in this world of satellites and multi-sites, the rural church is going virtual at the same time that it is getting very personal. BNC gets that, and we are ready to share the journey with others who are ready to break some rules to impact rural America and the world.

You know where to find us.

10
WALLS

Lessons from the Jerusalem Wall:
Nehemiah Meets Nebraska

Therefore I stationed some of the people behind the lowest points of the wall at the exposed places, posting them by families, with their swords, spears and bows. . . . "Don't be afraid of them. Remember the Lord, who is great and awesome, and fight for your brothers, your sons and your daughters, your wives and your homes" (Neh. 4:13–14).

He is just one person. And he is alone. Standing before his king, he asks for favor and the freedom to do the unthinkable: Nehemiah believes God has called him to rebuild the walls of Jerusalem, walls which his captor-king had actually destroyed. It is a dream — no, a vision — and Nehemiah knows it could cost him his life; it will certainly cost him his life as he knows it. But still, Nehemiah has no other choice.

He is just one person. And he is alone. Now he says he wants to rebuild a wall that is 3 feet deep, 16 feet tall, 4½ miles long, surrounding 960 acres, when the whole world is out to get this region — something that still hasn't changed throughout all of the ages. Jerusalem is still the target for many. It was the place where God resided, where the temple was, and everyone wanted it. Nehemiah, a palace slave, thought he could take it?

Impossible.

He is just one person. And he is alone. But this is a call, not an option. The people of Israel are scattered in exile, deprived of a place to worship, and wandering in spiritual darkness. The future of his people depends upon it. He could have denied the call and slithered back into complacent compliance. Or he could embrace the vision and see his people live, flourish, and worship the one true God.

Yes, he is just one person. And he is alone. It is the story of Nehemiah. It is also the story of Nebraska, of Iowa, of west Texas and Oklahoma . . . for this is the story of rural America and rural pastors wanting to give God their very best.

Exciting things happen when you transform one life after another. See beyond buildings, lights, and bigger facilities to discover the true power to grow your ministry in the video "Transformed Lives" at **www.nlpg. com/bnc.**

Daring to Dream

Now let me ask you a question: What is the dream, what is the vision that God has given you? Do you know? Do you not know? Do you know but have you put it on the back burner? What is the dream? Is it for your kids? Is it for an organization? Is it something huge? Is it something that seems huge only to you? I'm not asking just to be asking; this is not a rhetorical question. I'm asking you if you have a dream. There are no limits here, nothing specific. I know this is a book about growing the rural church, but this question is bigger than that. The dream might be something inside of you; it might be something huge out there. I don't know. All I know is that within the heart of every child of God is the desire to do great things for God. Within every heart of every child of God there are great things that are ready to come out. This is the heart of God, the God whose Spirit lives in us. He wants us to go forth and do big things for the cause of Christ. Do you have a dream? Do you know what it is?

God does.

Nehemiah's dream was ignited when he refused the urge to settle for the status quo. When he heard the news about how Jerusalem had been ravaged and left in ruins, he took the matter to his knees — a broken heart and a crying voice begging his Lord for something different:

> When I heard these things, I sat down and wept. For some days I mourned and fasted and prayed before the God of heaven. Then I said: "O LORD, God of heaven, the great and awesome God, who keeps his covenant of love with those who love him and obey his commands, let your ear be attentive and your eyes open to hear the prayer your servant is praying before you day and night for your servants" (Neh. 1:4–6).

Mourning, fasting, praying day and night . . . sometimes God-sized dreams and visions are revealed only after great struggle and great grief — broken hearts and voices crying out for change. What are the characteristics that are always found in people who dream God-sized dreams?

1. **Passion.** Nehemiah was a passionate man. He was a cupbearer. That means that he tasted everything the king was going to eat or drink. He could die every time he went to work. And I like to think that he was maybe just a tinge overworked. This has nothing to do with personality or fleshly charisma. Those things always fade away when the heat comes. Enthusiasm will fade away and those without it run for cover. The leader who has passion will barely yield.

2. **Motivation.** Motivation comes from the movement of God in our personal lives. When you are walking with God, in obedience to God, this is your motivation. You want to do things for Him, yet you know that they can only be accomplished by Him working through you. God is motivated by one thing: impossibility. If you are doing something average that you can do in your flesh, I believe that it cannot be of God. God wants something bigger than you, even though it might seem small and insignificant to everyone else.

3. **Discipline.** Disciplined people frustrate me. Their shirts are perfect, their checkbooks are balanced, their lawns always look great. . . . If you love discipline naturally, you are a very sick individual (my opinion, okay?! Ha ha!) But if God gives you a vision, He will give you the discipline to see it come to be. We see this in 1 Timothy: *The spirit of self-control is discipline.* Whatever your goal is, God is going to call you to discipline, and He will provide it if you trust in Him rather than in your own determination.

4. **Definition.** God works in obscurity, but His visions and dreams are generally very clear — even if He reveals them only one small step at a time. People with God-sized dreams can define them, articulate them, and write them down in

practical terms. People with God-sized dreams are practical and don't react or overreact. They just act. It's God's vision, it's God's will, and so they practically approach it in obedience.

Passion, motivation, discipline, and definition: if you think you have a God-sized dream, you're going to need to trust God to give you all four — because you're going to need them.

BNC Kids Area

Position of Opposition

Nehemiah's story is incredible history. If you want to know what it's like to grow a church in rural America, read the whole book, but particularly chapters 2 through 6. No matter what your dream is, Nehemiah shows what is required to follow through with God-sized dreams. I'm not sure where we got the idea that being a part of God's will in a fallen world should be peaceful, smooth sailing. It's just not that way. And boot the lie that says big churches have it any easier; scratch the idea that so-called success insulates you from struggle. It doesn't. When Satan tries to tell you that growth comes without pain, tell him to forget it. That's not in the Book. Moving ahead with a dream causes a big wake-up call when we run headlong into opposition of many kinds. Expect it!

Internal Opposition. When Nehemiah realized what his dream was, he also realized that he would have to stand before the most powerful man in the world to make it happen. On top of having a name that was entirely unpronounceable, King Artaxerxes was the ruler of the entire Babylonian and Persian

Empire. Just speaking to the king could cause him to lose his life, and yet Nehemiah knew that he must approach this man and not only ask for permission, but also for the provisions to fulfill his dream.

That would scare anybody, but my guess is that the fear of appearing before Artaxerxes was minuscule compared to the fear that Nehemiah had to overcome within himself. Yes, within every believer is a God-sized dream, but every believer wrestles with the stagnant, compromising, complacent instincts of the flesh that cause us to give in to the desire to settle for average. We settle for the culture, for second best, for compromise. We see what *we* are able to do, and we live according to that rather than going to the king and saying, "I am ready and I want you to pay for it."

Nehemiah didn't settle for what he could do, and the fear didn't derail the dream. When Jews were being paralyzed by fear of infiltration and attacked by those who wanted to end their work, Nehemiah exhorted them:

> Don't be afraid of them. Remember the Lord, who is great and awesome, and fight for your brothers, your sons and your daughters, your wives and your homes (Neh. 4:14).

Remember the Lord … remember the Lord … remember the Lord.

The internal opposition of fear is overcome only when we position ourselves to *remember the Lord.* Truly, none of this vision and dream stuff makes sense unless God Himself is in the picture. This is evident in the praise of the people who remembered the Lord in all that He had done after the wall had been rebuilt:

> Stand up and praise the Lord your God, who is from everlasting to everlasting. Blessed be your glorious name, and may it be exalted above all blessing and praise. You alone are the Lord. You made the heavens, even the highest heavens, and all their starry host, the earth and all that is on it, the seas and all that is in them. You give life to

everything, and the multitudes of heaven worship you (Neh. 9:5–6).

Yes, when fear comes, *remember the Lord.* The Lord of Nehemiah is *our* God; He's *your* God. He is the God of Pine Ridge, South Dakota, of Torrington, Wyoming, of Hammondsport, New York. He's even the God of South Lead Hill, Arkansas. So fear not.

External Opposition. As soon as your dream becomes public, you had better be ready for external attack. This happened to Nehemiah. "When Sanballat the Heronite, Tobiah the Ammonite official and Geshem the Arab heard about it, they mocked and ridiculed us. 'What is this you are doing?' They asked" (Neh. 2:19). In America, it's unlikely that external opposition will be physical; it's much more often psychological. You're ready to build, ready to make it happen. Then what happens? I guarantee it will be this: you have the vision, but when you have a dream, people are always in the wings ready to destroy it. All of a sudden, people with weird names are going to be in your lunch. Every time. Sand Ballet, Tofu, and Geekum, they are going to be there ready to squash it. They will be negative. They will doubt. They will make fun of you. They will call you an idiot. They will always try to draw you back.

People with little vision always go after people with big vision. In rural America, I call it "café-sized vision." Sand Ballet, Tofu, and Geekum: can't you see them leaning on the hood of their pickup truck? They've got their hats on and their sunglasses on top of the bill — they're all professional softball players on the side, you know — and they are laughing at you. "What is this thing you are doing?" They will scoff and wag their heads, and they will kill you if you let them. No, they won't kill your body. It's worse than that. They will kill your will. They will steal who you are so you will be just like them: neutered by the norm.

I'm telling you, watch out, because external opposition often comes from the people who are closest to you, from people who claim to have your best interests in mind, those who say they don't want you to get hurt or make a fool of yourself. They are the people at your right hand at the dinner table, the ones who are close enough to kiss you as you wrestle with your destiny in your own Garden of Gethsemane, the ones who have their hand on the money. . . . Yes, they are your Judas, the ones who greet you on the street with a smile and then stab you in the back in the barbershop. They might be your spouse or your kids or your mother or your college buddy. They might be the members of your own congregation, or the patron pastor at the church down the street who chuckles and rolls his eyes at your foolish faith. (Good luck, Sonny. You'll learn soon enough!)

Anytime God has called you to a bigger vision, there is always someone within arm's reach who will gently try to choke the dream out of you. With a wink and a nod they will draw you into doubt by causing you to forget the Lord and remember your fear — the exact opposite of what Scripture commands. But don't buy into it. External opposition is actually a confirmation. When you begin to live out a God-sized vision, it is guaranteed that people will start barking. When that happens you will know that this must be of God. And you might need to fight fire with fire. When they got in Nehemiah's face, he got back in theirs:

> I answered them by saying, "The God of heaven will give us success. We his servants will start rebuilding, but as for you, you have no share in Jerusalem or any claim or historic right to it" (Neh. 2:20).

How could he say that so confidently? Because he knew he was called, and he knew his vision was from God.

Physical Opposition. Nehemiah has rallied the troops, but in chapter 4 we see that they are starting to wear out. Because of the threats of imminent attack, they prayed and posted a guard day and night, putting an extra strain on their physical endurance. "The strength of the laborers is giving out, and there is so much rubble that we cannot rebuild the wall" (Neh. 4:10), the people cried out in exasperation.

I probably don't have to tell you how often this happens in the local church. In time, the pursuit of the dream loses its excitement, enthusiasm wanes, and it turns out that sometimes a work of God is, well, *work*. It's a vulnerable time, a time when the will to resist temptation runs low, and the desire for comfort and rest runs high. A time when maturity and obedience must override discouragement and disillusionment. It's a time when *enduring excellence* becomes a choice, when "vision" becomes an act of the will, rather than a response to an emotion.

It's a true test of leadership as well, and Nehemiah rose to the occasion. "The work is extensive and spread out, and we are widely separated from each other along the wall. Whenever you hear the sound of the trumpet, join us there. Our God will fight for us!" (Neh. 4:19–20). *Remember the Lord and remember the vision* is the trumpet call during such seasons. The wise leader will recognize the physical limitations of his laborers and will continue to project the dream while reminding the troops that the battle is the Lord's. When the troops are tired, we must remember the Lord, that He is the one who works within us and through us to conform us to His image, that we can trust in Him during those times when the spirit might be willing but the flesh becomes so weak.

Spiritual Opposition. And, oh yeah, there's the one who has come to steal, kill, and destroy (John 10). When opposition seems internal, external, and physical, we have to lift our eyes and look to the Word. To put opposition in perspective, we must remind ourselves that our struggle is not against flesh and blood, and that if we are to succeed we must take up the full armor of God in this war.

Because of the imminent attack by their enemies, Nehemiah commissioned half his men to work while the other half were "equipped with spears, shields, bows and armor. . . . Those who carried materials did their work with one hand and held a weapon in the other, and each of the builders wore his sword at his side as he worked" (Neh. 4:16–18). God help us that we should ever think that the opposition we face comes only from the opposition we can see. God help us that we should ever try to build a wall in our own strength thinking we can defend ourselves without taking up the armor of God.

Yes, opposition will come from inside and outside, from the weaknesses of the flesh, and from Satan. But that's just if you're a small struggling rural church. Once you establish VALUE, opposition evaporates, the road opens up, the way becomes smooth, the winds of change will be at your back, the clouds of struggle part, and the bright rays of sunshine beam down on you and your congregation.

Right?

Riiiiiiiiiiiiiight.

April Showers

I should be used to it by now, I guess — the opposition, that is. But I'm still blind-sided every time I think that we should be able to change and grow while sidestepping conflict. Just doesn't happen. It is still *change, conflict, growth,* no matter what size the church might be. I just have to smile and shake my head sometimes — it helps me get through the times when I break down and cry. I'm never amazed by the variety of struggles that come our way.

My son plays on a peewee ball team. Every time their bus passed our church to go to a game, the kids would boo right in front of my son. He has gotten used to it by now, but when it first started happening, he would ask, "Hey, dude, why are you booing my church?" And out of the mouths of his friends came echoes of the dinner time conversations around our community. "My grandparents say it's a cult," said one kid. "My dad said you have to show your W2 before you can join," announced another. (Sheesh. What fourth grade kid even knows what a W2 is?) Other people have said that I stole $500,000 dollars from the church. (If I did, will someone help me find it? I promise to tithe on it.) Yeah, I should be used to it by now, but it's extra hard when 95 percent of it comes from other Christians. I have been hammered and dragged through the mud, and that doesn't bother me nearly as much as the tragedy of the "he said, she said" junk that divides local churches, short-circuits our synergy, and stunts our growth.

Now, no matter what the size of the congregation, the same struggles show up. Never think that bigger is better or bigger is easier. Sometimes bigger is just harder. Because of budgeting issues and the dent in the economy, we recently had to release nine staff members. *Nine* of them. It was like tearing off our own arms and legs. Sometimes you have to amputate to save the body and that is what we had to do during that time. Still, my heart was broken and my ministry sails were lacking wind, but the church as a whole responded beautifully through encouragement, e-mails, even freezer jam (I love that stuff). Then six of the nine agreed to work with no pay so they could continue to enhance the vision. Totally blew me away. I mean, they hardly missed a beat and jumped back into the mission with all the passion and pure motivation of a volunteer. Some people really made a stink about it, but I also realized that the loudest boos usually come from those in the cheapest seats. As usual,

Cindy O'Dell

many outside our church misunderstood, blamed, feared, sowed discord, and made up stories in our small rural town. What do you do?

Once again, God showed me that nothing can or will stop His plan. In the weeks following the layoffs, the giving in our church went through the roof. Thank you again, Brand New Church, for your obedient giving and selflessness. So many gave, encouraged, and sacrificed for the continuing vision that we were able to slowly begin reinstating staff positions.

I thought maybe we had been through it all when last spring, storm clouds began to build over our staff team. When the funnel cloud dropped down, I felt like I was swept away in a tornado of confusion and chaos. My tears mixed with the spring rain during those months — weeks on end when nothing was clear, the fog descended, and all I knew was what I didn't know.

It started as I began to notice the dwindling job performance of one of our staff . . . a guy who was one of my best friends. He was eager and compliant enough on the outside, but he seemed so distracted and just wasn't following through with much of anything. It just didn't make sense. We had serious heart-to-hearts about it and he continued to assure me of his commitment — but his actions just weren't matching with his words. I finally sat down and I told him I was going to give him a couple of months to prove that I was planning on firing the wrong person. He promised me that would not be necessary. He assured me that he was still on board and would never hurt the church or me.

The next day a bloodbath of gossip raged through town. I walked into the local restaurant and everybody said, "Hey, I heard you fired ___." I was like, "How did you hear that?" "He was in here telling us!" they said. I was stunned. I felt like a three-year-old trying to put together a 500-piece puzzle. Nothing seemed to fit. But then it got worse. Rumors and misinformation started raging though the community about me and BNC — and all of it was coming from my friend. I did my best to not listen to the charges that were being leveled against me. I openly confess that I'm guilty of many things, but I simply could not accept the accusations that were being thrown my way. People started to take sides and many of our key families left for other churches.

I tried to defend Brand New Church and myself, but I felt I was shadowboxing with a ghost. Something was happening, but I couldn't get my hands on it. Nothing made sense . . . until the day I saw the bill for my friend's cell phone, a record that revealed a secret life of deceit and infidelity. As the trail of lies came into the light, they were met with denial on his part and devastation on his wife's part. When the facts could no longer be denied, they fractured the family, dazed his children, crushed the congregation, stunned our staff, shocked bystanders, and fueled plenty of gossip at the local bar. Everywhere I looked there were piles and piles of relational rubble left in the wake of the tornado of lies. And unfortunately, truth doesn't travel as fast as rumor and deception; damage is not repaired as fast as it is done, and sometimes it can't be repaired at all.

Looking Ahead

I have tried to get out of this job. I really have. My dream job is to own a Burger King. You laugh. Would you not love to own your own Burger King and get a triple whopper anytime you wanted? I would love that. I could just put in my time, hang out with high school kids all day, and collect my paycheck twice a month like I did back in Oklahoma City — and I would get extra cheese on all my burgers and wouldn't have to pay for it.

I simply can't do that — get out of this call to rural America, I mean. (Who knows, I might get to work at Burger King someday while I'm doing this, too!) I guess I'm just trying to tell you what I wasn't told when I signed up for this. Ministry in rural America takes place somewhere between nowhere and almost impossible. I had no idea how tough it would be, but I also never imagined what it would be like to be living inside a God-sized dream. Jesus tells it like it is:

> I have told you these things, so that in me you may have peace. In this world you will have trouble. But take heart! I have overcome the world (John 16:33).

There's a peace that comes with the turmoil. There's a filling that comes with the hunger. There's a healing that comes with the wounds. Yeah, God works in obscurity! There is just pure joy knowing that I'm living where I'm supposed to be, being who I was created to be, doing what I'm supposed to do. Sure, it costs, but it's absolutely priceless. Like Nehemiah building a wall so that his people could worship in peace, I just smile every time I think back to the nap that started it all. What started on a white couch at my in-laws' is now an unfolding reality: *together, we are all blazing a trail in rural America.*

No one can stop God's plan to advance His Church. Acts 5:38–39 says:

> If their purpose or activity is of human origin, it will fail. But if it is from God, you will not be able to stop these men; you will only find yourselves fighting against God.

We cannot fight against God's plan. He is leading you and me to reach those far from Him with greater passion and deeper sacrifice than ever before. It's all about God and for God. Like Nehemiah, God may have stationed us at the lowest places in the wall, the exposed places, far from the glitter and glam of metro Christianity. So be it.

> Remember the Lord, who is great and awesome, and fight for your brothers, your sons and your daughters, your wives and your homes (Neh. 4:14).

After the people had worked day and night for 52 days, Jerusalem was again in the hands of God's chosen — 52 days to complete four miles of wall and massive gates that the faithful could enter through. (Man, in the rurals, it would take 52 days just to get a bid!) But when God is in it, God does it. I so believe God wants to use you to do something so supernatural that you'll look back and know that it had to be Him. But it all starts with that first step — one step to start the journey. What is that step? God knows and He will take that step — and every step — with you, never forsaking you, never abandoning you as you "go out to the roads and country lanes and make them come in, so that my house will be full" (Luke 14:23). Jesus is making them come in, and God is doing some amazing things in small churches and communities in rural America. That's His nature. That's His business. And that's His history. As I look ahead, I have no idea of where the journey will take us next. But there are some things that I pray will never change.

Some Things Never Change

The Vision . . . that we would continue to reach rural America like never before, using every tool entrusted to us

The Passion . . . that we would live and preach the gospel with more intensity

The Mission . . . that we would network with all like-minded leaders who resist the urge to settle by growing the congregants of today to be the servant-leaders of tomorrow

The Message . . . that repentance, redemption, and transformed lives are what grow Christ's Church through Jesus' message

Why?

Because God is transforming church in rural America.

Because we hope that somehow, some way, you will join in this journey.

Because once there were rules.

And God has broken them.

So now . . .

May the God of peace, who through the blood of the eternal covenant brought back from the dead our Lord Jesus, that great Shepherd of the sheep, equip you with everything good for doing his will, and may he work in us what is pleasing to him, through Jesus Christ, to whom be glory for ever and ever. Amen (Heb. 13:20–21).

A thriving kids' ministry is what helped to fuel our growth at Brand New Church. Watch "The Future" at **www.nlpg.com/bnc** *to learn why providing quality worship for children must be a nonnegotiable.*

APPENDIX

Video Links

www.nlpg.com/bnc

Websites

www.brandnewchurch.com

www.breakingalltherurals.com

Connecting...
WITH SHANNON

facebook. ➡	www.facebook.com/shannonodell
twitter ➡	www.twitter.com/shannonodell
BLOG ➡	www.breakingalltherurals.com
WEBSITE ➡	www.brandnewchurch.com

With a passion for ministry in rural America, I am excited about the opportunity to connect and network with other pastors. In the last seven years as senior pastor of Brand New Church in the small community of Bergman, AR, I have been blessed to see incredible growth and transformation in this ministry. I encourage you to share ideas with other pastors in your community, and I would love to hear how God is working in your ministry. If you have questions or want to know more about what Brand New Church is doing, contact me.